PENGUIN BOOKS

DEGH TO DASTARKHWAN

Dr Tarana Husain Khan is a writer and cultural historian. Her writings on the oral history, culture and the famed cuisine of the erstwhile princely state of Rampur have appeared in prominent publications such as *Al Jazeera*, *Eaten Magazine*, *Scroll.in* and in the anthologies *Desi Delicacies* (Pan Macmillan, India) and *Dastarkhwan: Food Writing from South Asia and Diaspora* (Beacon Books, UK). She is the author of the historical fiction *The Begum and the Dastan*, which won the Kalinga Literary Award for fiction and was shortlisted for Women Writer's Award by She The People and longlisted for Auther Award.

She is currently working on a Research Fellowship at the University of Sheffield for an Arts and Humanities Research Council funded project 'Forgotten Food: Culinary Memory, Local Heritage and Lost Agricultural Varieties in India'.

ADVANCE PRAISE FOR THE BOOK

'Powerful food stories run deep in our country's rich heritage, and this book is a wonderful example that if you do the research, it truly does pay off. Peppered with food memories, anecdotes and unique recipes from Rampur and its largely forgotten, grand cuisine, this is the kind of culinary documentation that leaves you salivating on so many levels.'

—Thomas Zacharias,
Chef and Founder of The Locavore

'Beautifully captured the essence and contribution of Rampuri Cuisine. Rampur has a legacy of a very bold style of food by some legendary khansamas of the time. Tarana ji has brought to light the stories, recipes and the thought behind the cuisine of a bygone era.'

—Kunal Kapur,
Chef and Restaurateur

'Tarana casts a powerful spell by writing about foods that memories are made of. Boundaries blur between the past and the present, and wafting aromas transport us like a magic carpet would to lands and people that no longer exist. Blissfully, she shares recipes that will help us recreate this magic, even if partially. *Degh to Dastarkhwan* is meticulously researched and written with a refreshingly light touch. A gem!'

—Pushpesh Pant,
Food Critic and Historian

DEGH TO DASTARKHWAN

QISSAS *and* RECIPES *from* RAMPUR

Tarana Husain Khan

PENGUIN BOOKS

An imprint of Penguin Random House

PENGUIN BOOKS

USA | Canada | UK | Ireland | Australia
New Zealand | India | South Africa | China

Penguin Books is part of the Penguin Random House group of companies
whose addresses can be found at global.penguinrandomhouse.com

Published by Penguin Random House India Pvt. Ltd
4th Floor, Capital Tower 1, MG Road,
Gurugram 122 002, Haryana, India

Penguin
Random House
India

First published in Penguin Books by Penguin Random House India 2022

Copyright © Tarana Husain Khan 2022

10 9 8 7 6 5 4 3 2

ISBN 9780143451464

Typeset in Goudy Old Style by Manipal Technologies Limited, Manipal
Printed at Replika Press Pvt. Ltd, India

www.penguin.co.in

For Rampur's legendary khansamas, who endure in
the culinary memories and oral history of Rampur

Dar kami-o-peshi ikhtiyaar-e-hast.
The balance of everything [flavours] is in our hands.
—*Khwan e Neymat*

Jo kha liya wo apna hai
We eat what our destiny granted us.[1]
(a quaint Rampuri idiom)

---

[1] The saying exemplifies the contented temperament of Rampur people. What we lack was never destined for us.

Contents

Author's Note

I did not identify myself as a culinary connoisseur or an aficionado of Rampuri cuisine. Let me confess that I come from a long line of non-cooking gourmands and armchair food critics of both sexes. When my grandmother called the cook and chastened him for being lazy and not sautéing the masalas properly and for adding too much or too little of some spice, instructing him on some delicate nuance that he missed out on, it became a part of my subconscious education in the cuisine. My taste buds and senses learned from every satisfactory, delicious and dissatisfying dish. Equally amusing were the food stories around the dishes, the culinary colloquialisms and idioms. Though my grandparents had shifted from Rampur to Aligarh with their young brood in the sixties, their tastes, lifestyles and food belonged to the erstwhile princely state. In our house it was an unquestionable fact that Rampur cuisine was several notches above the over-aromatic Awadhi cuisine or the opulent Mughal cuisine.

It was by a stroke of luck that I came across a treasure trove of cookbook manuscripts dating back to the nineteenth century at the Raza Library at Rampur. The script was Persian, and I could only read the names of the dishes. Browsing through the vast repertoire of dishes, I realized that we had forgotten several culinary masterpieces from a carefully honed and curated cuisine of the princely state of Rampur. Thus began the journey of my culinary consciousness fuelled by a desire to put Rampur back on the culinary map of India.

Rampur was a teardrop of a princely state established by Rohilla Pathans in 1774 under the British colonial rule. It rose into prominence and became a centre of north Indian Muslim culture, especially after the destruction of Delhi and Lucknow after the rebellion of 1857. Stationed between the two fallen giants of Muslim culture, Delhi and Awadh, Rampur was prosperous enough to absorb the destitute artists, musicians, poets and chefs fleeing the destruction after 1857. Today, the culinary manifestation of Rampur is the most popular and the most enduring aspect of Rampur's culture even though several facets of the gastronomic greatness have been forgotten. This book attempts to recapture the culinary spectrum of Rampur's foodway, lay out its abiding legacy and answer the question—what constitutes and distinguishes the Rampuri cuisine. It also delves into the oral and written history of the cuisine, its quirky and emotional food memories and cultural practices around food, drawing the reader into the warmth of 'Rampuriyat'. Food becomes a reflection of a people, a lens to view the city, its culinary history and a metaphor of emotional memories lived and narrated.

Each chapter represents an emotion, an observance, or a celebration. The spread of Rampuri food from the grand to the humble—the quotidian Rampuri dastarkhwan—becomes the arena to express love, loss, forgiveness and spirituality. Thus, qorma celebrates weddings, pulao comforts the mourners, kababs invite forgiveness and andarsas welcome monsoons.

The book is peopled with compelling characters from all walks of life and their food stories. It quotes a Rampur princess as she reminiscences the grand feasts at her father's palace and how a guest nearly died of overeating at a royal banquet. The journey of a khansama from the royal kitchens to humbler abodes mirrors the slow crumbling of a meticulously curated cuisine; the spiritual ambience and langar at the Sufi shrine of Shah Baghdadi recall the qawwali mehfils at my great grandfather's grave. Connecting food memories and oral history around the food culture of Rampur, each chapter ends with an authentic recipe from Rampuri homes and old khansamas.

Investigating the history of Rampur cuisine, gathering food stories and learning the nuances of finely cooked Rampuri dishes made me discover a latent part of myself. Maybe I didn't consciously care about food while growing up, but I could appreciate the taste of good food; I could recall a perfect meal with great joy and I strove to recreate certain tastes of my childhood. This possibly makes me a foodie in denial. While I cannot pretend to be an authority on Rampur cuisine, I believe, like all cuisines, it has followed a trajectory of cultural amalgamations, everyday transformations—in royal kitchens, humble homes, through interactions between khansamas and their masters and mistresses—which have survived in the form of food stories and emotional memories connected to the larger narrative of the colony and the nation. I have tried to focus on the written histories of royal cuisine, the hidden oral histories and the voices in the kitchens—the khansamas and the ladies of the house—the layered gastro nostalgia replete with the textures and the intimacies of preparation and eating of food.

Cooking Notes

The experienced cook goes on auto pilot and every ingredient is added with the fuzzy cooking intelligence of andaza—an approximation. The dish in different hands tastes different; it is *haath ka mazaa*, the individual cooking style. As it says in the ancient cookbook—'the excess and paucity of everything is in our hand'. This is true for cooking and for life in general. I'm not a regular cook, and for me, cooking is some andaza and some faltering—'add in, taste and then add some more' kind of an exercise. So, reducing the andaza to specific quantities of ingredients took some time, and I would still recommend invoking your inner cooking wisdom; I'm sure in your hands the preparations will carry your unique style.

The recipes in this book, which I tried and modified, are collected from various sources—khansamas, aunts, friends and old cookbooks. Most of the dishes are cooked in Rampur homes today with some variations. I realized that even if the readers are experienced in Indian cooking, some finer points should be put forth for their convenience.

1. The cooking medium that I prefer is either ghee or well-smoked mustard oil. Often, cooks and gourmands use vegetable ghee or refined oil when they make pulaos and curries on formal or celebratory occasions.

2. Rampuri cuisine, as all Muslim cuisines, has a proclivity towards the excessive use of ghee or oil; one can make do with less oil than the amount I have mentioned in the recipes.

3. In Rampur, we use dried yellow chillies in most of the preparations. Red chilli powder is used in curries for colour. In case yellow chillies are not available, one can substitute with red chillies. In curries, we generally use both red and yellow chillies in the proportion of 2:1. Our food is very spicy, so please use chillies as per your tolerance of the spice.

4. Most of the curry recipes are for a kilogram of meat. In case you want to cook half a kilogram, the ingredients are not reduced by half but by three quarters. To demonstrate this, I have given one recipe of qorma for half a kilogram. Some other recipes are also for half a kilogram of meat. The measurement of spices is not sacrosanct but an indication. Invoke your inner andaza.

5. Coriander powder is not used in large quantities in Rampuri curries as it is in other cuisines. Rampuris feel it makes the curry darker and changes the taste. If you want more curry, the easiest thing is to increase the amount of coriander by one or two teaspoons.

6. In the ingredient list, please be mindful of teaspoon (tsp) and tablespoon (tbsp)!

7. If parched gram powder is not available, you can dry grind parched gram (bhuna chana). If nothing else, sauté besan on a skillet.

8. In Rampur, we use the basic whole garam masalas. For the garam masala powder, you can use the store brought garam masala of a good brand, but it is preferable to prepare the following masala powders:

    • For aromatic masala powder, dry grind 5 grams each of nutmeg, star anise, cinnamon and mace.

    • For garam masala powder, dry grind 10 grams each of cloves, black peppercorns, cumin seeds with 10 black cardamoms and 20 green cardamoms.

You can add everything together and have an aromatic garam masala!

One

Pulao and Mourning

Pulao, an aromatic rice and meat dish, has a seminal presence in all traditional Muslim households. No feast, funeral or prayer meeting is complete without it. In Rampur, the timing of serving the pulao is crucial. The partakers are supposed to wait for it at the table while it is put on dum—simmering in a dough-sealed pot or cooker. The literal translation of dum is life. The pulao becomes lifeless when the dum steam escapes.

It would be inconceivable for most people to associate the lavish pulao with mourning and remembrances. Pulaos take me back to Thursday fatihas (prayers) in my ancestral home in Aligarh. While growing up, we associated Thursdays with pulao lunch. My siblings, cousins and I could almost smell the pulao as our rickshaw wheeled us slowly back from school. Lunch would invariably be served late, for several kilos of pulao had to be prepared in a large degh (large cooking vessel with a narrow mouth) over wood fire in the old kitchen, with Zarina Bua, our cook, muttering over the quality of meat or rice, ready to blame the lack of perfection on our old retainer, Khalil Khan. The pulao was distributed to the poor after remembrance prayers to invoke blessings for our ancestors.

In the sixties, my grandparents with their brood of nine children had migrated from Rampur to Aligarh, where my grandfather had taken up an assignment as the university engineer at Aligarh Muslim University. Their taste buds were still Rampuri, and they created an ecosystem of foodways from Rampur—khansamas, rice, wheat, masalas and seasonal fruits. My grandmother had banished all the Sufi practices from her house after the death of her mother-in-law—Nani Amma came from a family that had a puritan Islamic belief system—but fortunately retained the reading of the Thursday fatiha over steaming dishes of pulao as remembrance-prayers for her husband and ancestors. It was one of the traditions she carried from her Rampur life. We—aunts, uncles, parents, cousins and siblings—would surround the dining table with our palms raised heavenwards, heads covered respectfully, stomachs rumbling as Nani Amma recited the Quranic verses and prayed for everlasting peace in Jannat for the dead buzurgs. We recited the prayers under our breath, at least I did; most kids just stared at the food.

My grandmother believed that the spirits of the dead, particularly her husband's, came down on Thursdays, and so prayers of remembrance had to be recited over a sample of steaming pulao dish before we began to eat. It always confused us as children—were the spirits hungry or did they just come down to eat pulao? We were not allowed to question our elders once we had passed a certain age. The prayed over and the now holy pulao was taken away and mixed into the degh (to make it all holy) and we finally got to eat, though not before a large portion was taken out for the maulvi of the neighbouring mosque and the poor living beyond our area of reference.

Over the years, as Nani Amma became ill and passed the supervision of the kitchen to the daughters-in-law, the quantity of pulao reduced, the degh was replaced by a large pan, which could be used for cooking on the gas stove instead of the open wood fire in the courtyard. The fatiha prayer was still said over the pulao dish and a nashteydaan was sent to the maulvi of the neighbouring mosque. Nani Amma is no more with us; we still have pulaos on Thursdays, but there are no prayers for ancestors. Fatiha now belongs to a class of religious traditions which are declared 'bida' or innovations to be studiously avoided by those following the pure, unalloyed religion.

My childhood association with pulao and prayers, the memory of pulao smells overlaid with incense fragrance, is reinforced by the serving of the dish at funerals. At a Rampur funeral, the timing of serving the pulao is even more critical. The funeral bier is borne out of the house on the shoulders of grim-faced mourners, leaving behind a gaggle of crying, wailing and sniffing women. When the men return from the close-by burial ground—there is a sense of calm resignation that borders on satisfaction if the dead person was old and ailing—and grief has subsided to a contained level, a cart bearing deghs of pulao trundles through the brick-laid lane, and pulao deghs are carried into the courtyard. Suddenly, there is a change in the tone of the day as morose-looking women get busy serving the piping hot feast to comfort the mourners. The perfect timing never ceases to amaze me; even in mourning it is crucial that the pulao should be served before all its steaming life, dum, escapes. Even in devastating grief one cannot serve cold pulao.

Recently, the Rampuris have started spicing up the pulao with yellow chilli flakes and whole green chillies to suit the local palate. The old-timers (and I) still prefer the delicate redolence of the dish with a tiny amount of yellow chilli chutney and the occasional dahi phulki (fritters in curd).

The Rampur cuisine now has a basic yakhni pulao prepared with hybrid Basmati rice and with the yakhni (meat stock) as its base. Till the nineties, the rice used for pulao was Hans Raj, a local heritage rice with unparalleled aroma. Hans Raj is now practically extinct, but the old-timers remember the aroma of pulao wafting throughout the mohalla enticing some brazen neighbours to drop in and ask for a plateful. The rice grains of Hans Raj were smaller than those of Basmati, which seduced us with its curving length. The old gourmands, however, often complain that the long grains stick in their throats and taste like plastic. The fetish for white rice with each grain standing elegantly separate, coated in ghee, is a Persian import. Indians used to eat brown and black unpolished rice till the Persians convinced us to soak the rice in saltwater to make it pristine white. The hybrid Basmati is almost devoid of natural fragrance and is dependent upon spices and meat stock to grant it the all-important pulao redolence.

The Rampuris love their yakhni pulao and turn up their noses at the richer and spicier version, the biryani, which has become the most popular rice and meat dish across

India. The biryani is rebuffed by the Rampuris as a soulless mixture of qorma layered with semi-boiled rice. The cooking procedures are totally different; the base for pulao is the meat stock, and it is closer to the original Persian version; on the other hand, biryani is prepared by layering spicy meat curry with boiled rice and putting it on dum. Food historian Lizzie Collingham writes in *Curry: A Tale of Cooks and Conquerors* that the delicately flavoured Persian 'pilaf' met the rich, spicy Mughal dishes in the kitchens of Emperors Humayun and Akbar to create the biryani. The Mughal chefs marinated the meats in yoghurt and spices, cooked it and layered it with boiled-and-strained rice and dough-sealed the pot in the manner of the Mughal technique of dumpukht. Until my recent gastronomic enlightenment, I used the terms pulao and biryani interchangeably, as most people do. This is an error bordering on culinary blasphemy—the two are vastly different in taste and texture.

I'm not a foodie or a recipe fanatic; or, maybe, I am in denial. So, it was by sheer luck that I came upon about a 150-year-old Persian cookbook manuscript at the Raza Library in Rampur while researching for my novel. The Raza Library, renowned all over the world for its manuscript collection, is housed in Hamid Manzil, the erstwhile court of the Nawabs of Rampur, and peopled with crusty librarians who guard the ancient manuscripts with self-righteous doggedness. The gentleman in charge of the manuscript section—a caricature of a librarian with his stiff, white threatening beard, scrawny frame and thick glasses—sits in a gloomy room surrounded by huge steel almirahs with their precious stacks. He is only affable towards scholars who come armed with the knowledge of Persian; I could just manage basic Urdu. He had banned one of the research scholars from assessing the recipe manuscripts because he found him too casual. The researcher chanced upon me pottering around, trying to find clues to the vanishing culture of Rampur and handed me the names of the recipe manuscripts that held the key to pulaos, kababs and qormas.

As Rampur is also renowned for its culinary culture, I presented myself to the librarian asking for the manuscript. He looked at me with disdain over his rickety, steel-framed spectacles, asked me the Persian word for the art of cooking and, sure enough, found me wanting, so summarily dismissed me. Small towns have a deep respect for connections and genealogy and, very soon, I found myself back in the inner sanctum of the library—this time to face the slightly mellowed librarian.

'Why didn't you tell me that you are the granddaughter of Jabbar Khan engineer?' he demanded, a bit miffed at being commanded by the director to assist me. My grandfather, Abdul Jabbar Khan, belonged to the family of first Rohilla settlers of Rampur (1774) and was the riyasat engineer till the merger of Rampur state in 1949. Thus, the treasured manuscripts were revealed to me, and I was allowed to make copies.

The cookbook manuscripts are thin volumes, closely handwritten in Persian, dating from 1816 till the end of the nineteenth century, spanning the era of three Nawabs of Rampur. Some bear the names of authors—who were possibly gourmets and members of nobility—and scribes, and were probably commissioned by the Nawabs while the others were transcripts and copies of the original manuscripts. Just as we collect glossy cookbooks, the Nawabs collected or commissioned these handwritten cookbooks. They were aspirational models or reference books for the gourmet Nawabs who wished to elevate the simple tribal cuisine of the Rohillas to an instrument of gastrodiplomacy. Interestingly, they were all written in Persian, the language of the educated aristocrats, which could not be read or understood by the khansamas. Possibly the Nawab told the kitchen munsarim (administrator) to get, for instance, Pulao Shahjahani for a special occasion; a courtier was asked to read and translate the recipe for the khansama. Such imagined scenarios and conversations flashed through my mind as I attempted to read the names of bewildering styles of pulaos, kababs and qormas.

As I studied the cookbook manuscripts in the context of historical writings on Rampur culture, I was able to conclude that by the beginning of the nineteenth century, the Nawabs of Rampur had commenced a process of gentrification in all aspects of culture. The major influencer in the process was the Awadhi Muslim subculture. Najmul Ghani Khan in his historical account *Akhbar us Sanadeed* laments the influence of Awadhi culture as the Pathan shalwar-kameez gave way to Awadhi kurta-pyjama. In the context of cuisine, the Nawabs started developing and innovating a more elegant and comprehensive culinary repertoire, working on the basic meat curries, pulaos, as well as the tribal qaliya from Afghani foodways. Thus, the collection of handwritten cookbook manuscripts, which I stumbled upon at the Raza Library, date from the time of Nawab Sayed Ahmed Ali Khan (ruled 1794–1840) and show the culinary aspirations of the Nawab.

The transformation in culture was further reinforced by the exodus of artists and chefs from the destroyed cultural centres of Delhi and Awadh after the rebellion of 1857. The

Nawabs welcomed and employed writers, artist, poets and chefs from the fallen kingdoms of Delhi and Awadh. The cooks from these cultural centres were employed at the royal kitchens and collaborated with their Rampur counterparts to craft the inimitable Rampuri royal cuisine. Thus, Rampur survived the devastating consequences of the rebellion of 1857 and became the cultural node of north Indian Muslim culture as well as the culinary ethos.

Nawab Hosh Yaar Jung Bilgrami, a courtier from 1918 till 1928 at the durbar of Nawab Sayed Hamid Ali Khan (ruled 1894–1930), writes in his account *Mashahidaat* that there were 150 cooks in the royal kitchens, each specializing in creating only one dish. 'Such cooks could not be found with the Mughal emperors or in Iran, Turkey and Iraq.' He writes of at least 200 dishes, including English and Middle Eastern fare, cooked at a banquet hosted by Nawab Sayed Hamid Ali Khan.

There was a separate rice kitchen at the Nawab of Rampur's Khasbagh Palace and the khansamas were legendary in creating the most exquisite and innovative rice dishes. Begum Jahanara Habibullah in her memoir—on the princely state of Rampur and on the years after independence— *Remembrance of Days Past*, writes of ten varieties of pulao served at Nawab Sayed Raza Ali Khan's (ruled 1930–1949) tables till the 1960s. Dumpukht pulao made with whole partridge, quail, chicken or a leg of mutton is a Rampur speciality. Most Rampuri homes today cook the basic yakhni pulao. The grand repertoire of fifty-odd styles of the pulao in the manuscript is very intriguing. It ranges from the grand Pulao Shahjahani, the sweet pulaos—mutanjan pulao (sweet pulao with meat), pulao sheer shakkar (milk and sugar)—to the ananas (pineapple) pulao, imli (tamarind) pulao, etc. Most of these varieties are unheard of and a few endure as food memories. Begum Jahanara writes of ananas pulao, with a lifelike pineapple created out of sugar, and anar pulao, with a pomegranate presented on the rice.

Fascinated, I decided to learn basic Persian, took the help of Mr Isbah Khan from the library and started translating these extinct gastronomic delights. Isbah Khan, a younger and kinder version of the manuscript librarian, introduced me to an old Rampuri khansama (chef) to make sense of the recipes. The original cooks of the court are no more, and their children have taken up different professions.

I decided to cook Pulao Shahjahani, a dish probably imported from Mughal cuisine, which was described in most of the manuscripts. The khansama and I were confused and confounded at many levels while going through the recipes. The ingredients were measured in daam, tola, masha, ratti and ser—ancient measures with inexact modern equivalents; they are preceded by dots, dashes and slashes—symbols which hold no meaning even for the old-timers. At one point, I found myself measuring out 550 gm of cinnamon for 1 kg pulao! It was absurd.

Measurements were the least of my worries. The procedures outlined in the recipes are brief and cryptic, as though making presumptions about our knowledge of cooking. The cooking terminology had also changed over time.

When it becomes thick, add meat and some proper masala and keep watching . . .

Temper the meat with yakhni water. Boil rice in water after putting meat. Evaporate half the shorba. Separate yakhni into two parts.

What was 'yakhni' and what was 'shorba'? Could they be used interchangeably? What was the 'proper masala'? There were procedures within procedures and changing of deghs many times during the process of cooking. In Pulao Shahjahani, one ends up with four vessels to be washed afterwards. No wonder, with time, we abbreviated the whole intricate procedure into a two-step affair and replaced the degh with the trusty pressure cooker.

I was on the verge of giving up the venture when I chanced upon two recipe books on Mughal cuisine, printed in Delhi dating back to 1873 and 1879, which have the elusive Pulao Shahjahani with the procedure more clearly explained. It was like coming upon the Rosetta stone! The 'yakhni' has meat boiled with spices, and when the meat is removed, the leftover water is called 'shorba'. I could finally decode this fascinating recipe.

I finally managed to cook Pulao Shahjahani with the khansama, and it turned out to be as elegant and opulent as its name.

The recipe ends with the somewhat philosophical line:

Dar kami-o-peshi ikhtiyaar-e-hast.

The balance of everything (flavours) is in our hands.

Yakhni Pulao Shahjahani

As discussed earlier, this is an ancient recipe. It tastes grand.

Ingredients

1/2 kg mutton
1 kg rice
2 cups of ghee
100 gm almond, blanched and skinned
1/2 cup curd
2 inch cinnamon stick
15 cloves
20 green cardamoms
3-4 black cardamoms
1 tsp green cardamom powder
2 tsp cumin seeds
2 tsp black peppercorns
4 medium onions
1 tbsp garlic paste
2 tbsp coriander seeds
1 tsp garam masala powder
1 tsp saffron
Lahori salt to taste

Method

1. Soak the rice in water for about half an hour. Grind the coriander seeds to a thick paste. Grind skinned almonds to a paste.

2. Put the meat with half of the finely cut onions, 1 tablespoon ghee, half of the coriander paste and about 2.5 to 3 litres of water in a deghchi to make yakhni. Keep on boiling till the meat becomes tender. If pressure cooker is used, add only about 1.5 litres of water.

3. Take out the meat from the yakhni. Sieve the water.

4. For tempering, take 1 tablespoon of ghee, add seeds of 10 cardamoms and about 5 cloves. Heat it till cloves become reddish, then put into the yakhni. Keep it aside.

5. In another deghchi, heat the rest of the ghee (leaving about 100 gm). Add the remaining finely diced onions. When the onions are golden fried, add cloves and cardamoms. Then add the meat. Stir till the meat is well coated with ghee.

6. Add the remaining coriander and garlic pastes and stir. Add ground almond paste and curd. Add garam masala powder and cardamom powder to the gravy.

7. Keep cooking till a little gravy is left, the ghee separates and the meat is tender.

8. Boil the rice in water till it is about half done. It should be firm. Sieve the rice grains in a colander to remove excess water and soak in the yakhni prepared earlier, for about 15 minutes.

9. For the final preparation, put all the spices on the meat, take the rice out of the yakhni and lay it on top of the meat. Add just enough yakhni to cover the rice since the rice is nearly cooked. Cover the deghchi and seal with kneaded flour so that no steam can escape. Simmer for about 15 minutes. This is dum.

10. After opening the deghchi, spread some ghee on top. Soak saffron in warm water and sprinkle this water and saffron threads over the pulao. Serve hot.

Yakhni Pulao Khaas

This is an elaborate version of yakhni pulao we prepare in our homes. Skip the almonds, cream and bones if you want the regular pulao.

Ingredients

1 kg fine Basmati rice[1]
1 large cup well-smoked mustard oil or refined oil or 250 gm ghee
1/2 kg mutton[2]
1/2 kg bones (optional)
100 gm almonds, blanched and finely cut (optional)
1 cup cream (optional)
1 tbsp garlic paste
3–4 medium-sized garlic bulbs
2 large onions, diced finely
2 inch piece of ginger, chopped
2 tsp fennel seeds
2 tsp coriander seeds
1/2 cup curd

---

[1] The proportion of meat to rice can vary from 1:2 to 1:1 depending on personal preferences.
[2] Cooks advocate using the meat of a young animal. Some khansamas prefer shoulder meat and ribs. Leg meat is good too. Basically, the meat should not be lean as the fat makes the pulao rich. Some cooks use an equal amount of meat and rice, which makes a richer pulao.

6 bay leaves
10 cloves
10 green cardamoms
1 inch cinnamon stick
1/2 cup milk
Juice of two lemons
Salt to taste

Method

1. Wash the meat and bones properly. Wash and soak the rice for 30 minutes.
2. In a large pan, take a tablespoon of ghee (or well-smoked mustard oil, but ghee is best) and fry a quarter of diced onions till golden. Add meat and bones. Pour in 3 litres of water. Add chopped ginger, pods of garlic, fennel seeds, coriander seeds and 1 teaspoon of salt. Boil till meat becomes tender and approximately less than a litre of water remains. If using a pressure cooker, 1 to 1 1/2 litres of water will do. Discard the bones; keep the meat aside. Sieve the water. This is the yakhni. If you plan to cook without bones, halve the amount of water.
3. In a wide-mouthed vessel, add the remaining ghee and fry the onions and take them out when golden. Add cardamoms, cinnamon, cloves and meat. Fry the meat while adding ground garlic and curd till the smell of garlic goes away. Add salt and lemon juice. Pour in the cream and let it simmer till the oil separates and floats to the top.
4. Add rice and fry a little. Pour in yakhni water till it stands about 1 inch above the rice. Check the salt. If some stock

is left, you can freeze it and use it while cooking vegetable pulao, pea pulao, etc.

5. Boil on high heat till the rice is nearly done. Add milk and continue to boil for a minute.

6. Lower the heat, add fried onions, finely cut almonds and saffron water and seal the cover with a wet cloth or dough. Put on low simmer for about 10 minutes and remove from heat. If using a pressure cooker, add less water and only 1/4 cup milk. The rice should not become too soggy. Use your judgement.

7. Serve hot with garlic and chilli chutney.

* This can be made with chicken too. For chicken, when boiling yakhni, do not add the chicken pieces, just boil the spices till less than a litre of water is left. Chicken is cooked till it becomes tender before the rice is put in (Step 3).

Yakhni Pulao Saada

A simple and quick yakhni pulao if you don't have much time but are craving pulao.

Ingredients

1/2 kg mutton
1 kg rice
1 cup ghee

8 cloves
10 green cardamoms
1 tsp black peppercorns
5–6 bay leaves
1 tsp cumin seeds
1 cup cream
1/2 cup milk
3 medium onions, finely diced
1 tbsp garlic paste
1 tbsp ginger paste
Salt to taste

Method

1. Wash and soak the rice for at least 15 minutes.
2. Wash the meat. Take half of the ginger–garlic paste and mix well with the meat.
3. Fry finely cut onions in the ghee till they become golden. Add meat into it and sauté till the oil becomes visible on top and the water evaporates.
4. Now add cream and milk, and mix.
5. Add all the spices and let this boil till the meat becomes tender.
6. Put in the rice and adequate water and let it boil. In a pressure cooker, the water should stand about an inch above the rice. More water is needed for a pan. Cover the pan with a wet cloth under the lid or seal lid with dough. Put on low simmer for about 10 minutes and remove from heat.
7. When the rice is almost done, keep on low heat for dum till it is completely done but not overcooked. In a pressure

cooker, turn off the flame after three whistles and keep the lid closed till it cools down.

Qorma Pulao

This is an old recipe, much like biryani. It might have been called 'qorma pulao' earlier.

Ingredients

1/2 kg meat
1 kg rice
250 gm ghee
6–7 cloves
10 green cardamoms
2–3 black cardamoms
2 inch cinnamon stick
1 tsp black peppercorns
1/2 tsp saffron
2 tsp coriander powder
2 tsp ginger paste
1 tbsp garlic paste
3–4 medium onions, finely diced
1 tsp cumin seeds
1–2 tsp red chilli powder
1 1/2 cup curd
Salt to taste

Method

1. Wash and soak rice.
2. Marinate the meat with salt, curd and ginger–garlic pastes for half an hour.
3. Heat half of the ghee and fry the onions till golden. Remove half of the fried onions.
4. Add marinated meat and fry till it becomes reddish, then add coriander and red chilli powder.
5. Add water to make the meat tender.
6. When the meat is almost done, add half of the fried onions set aside earlier.
7. Add powdered cloves, cardamoms, peppercorns, cumin seeds and cinnamon (or 2 tsp garam masala powder) and let it simmer till the fried onions are completely mixed into the gravy. The gravy should be smooth. Add more water, if required.
8. Drain the rice. Put in a pan with remaining fried onions, cover with water (about an inch above the rice) and boil till almost done. It should be firm. Sieve the rice grains in a colander to remove excess water.
9. Make two alternating layers of meat and rice.
10. Add the leftover ghee on top along with saffron water, seal pan and simmer till done.

Peeli/Lal Mirch Chutney

This is an important accompaniment to yakhni pulao since the pulao itself is of delicate flavour.

Ingredients

7–10 red (lal) or yellow (peeli) dried chillies
15 cloves of garlic
1/2 tsp cumin seeds
1tsp ghee
Salt to taste

Method

1. Grind the chillies, peeled garlic and cumin with some water. The texture should be thick and grainy. Grinding on stone sil-batta (stone mortar and pestle) with little water is preferable.
2. Add salt.
3. Heat the ghee in a pan and fry the chutney. This step is optional.
4. Serve with yakhni pulao and kababs.

Two

Weddings and the Repletion of Taar Roti and Qorma

The arrival of *Amreeka wali nani* signalled the beginning of the family wedding season. Fuelled with countless cups of tea and cigarettes, her chief sustenance, the formidable lady set to work: 'hitching the unhitchable', pairing off recalcitrant, unemployed grandnephews with potential heiresses, lending an open purse to cash-strapped relatives and smoothening overall objections on any matter with her loud, raspy voice. Suddenly there was hope everywhere in the ancient houses edging the narrow gullies as she shuffled her spry, slightly bent form from one house to the next, forging and forcing alliances with tremendous velocity. For *Amreeka wali nani*, the institution of marriage was based on two premises—it could solve most problems, and its success was based on withheld information. Once the alliance was fixed, she set to work— supervising the arrangements, enjoying the ceremonies and singing with the girls to the beat of the dhol. The bride's and the groom's families would quarrel over having her on their side, and she would bask in their attention, smiling beatifically. As all Rampuris, she loved taar roti—the most amazing meat curry served with tandoori roti—the dish that served as the culmination of the marriage events. She ate taar roti with such gusto that one assumed her dedication to fostering marital alliances rested on the edifice of her fanatic devotion to the iconic Rampur delicacy.

Taar roti is the main star of the walima—the reception banquet—which announces the nuptials to all, *khaas o aam*, the distinguished and the general populace. Traditionally, the banquet has a no-frills, one-dish menu—taar roti. The dessert is usually sweet rice or zarda. Some people add yakhni pulao (rice cooked in meat stock) or seekh kababs to the spread, but these are relegated to being side dishes. There are no drinks or salads to hamper the single-minded focus on the sublime culinary delight. The basic idea of this simplistic menu was to feed the entire tribe in celebration—and the tradition continues. The feast begins at around eleven in the morning and continues till around three in the afternoon. Nowadays, the walima is held more often at night in the glittering shadi ghars dotting the city. The nikah ceremony is generally a simple affair at the local mosque followed by distribution of sweets, and the walima is the main feast that everyone looks forward to. Though there has been a recent trend of a wedding feast with a large spread, it doesn't take the limelight away from the simple taar roti dawat relished by Rampuris.

In the ladies' section, the women struggle out of their abaya gowns,[1] hand over the congratulatory salami envelopes bearing the socially acceptable amount to the hostess, buzz through perfunctory socializing and make their way to the dining tables. Some hit the feast first, before it becomes too crowded, and handle the protocol later.

The taar roti is always a sit-down feast served in basic crockery. The pace is hectic as hot bowls of taar gravy are replaced as soon as they grow tepid; the fresh-from-the-oven khameeri roti (leavened bread), more than a foot in diameter, is broken into palm-sized pieces by the member of the family supervising the table and handed to the guest. As soon as it finishes, another piping hot piece is inserted into the outstretched hand. The legendary hospitality of the Pathans is on full display. The guests are just as discerning. They would feel slighted if the rotis are dumped in front of them or if the curry is not replaced. The comment is always on the taste of the curry and the dedication with which it was served. True connoisseurs can even identify the cook and the butcher. Recently, I feasted on an end-of-the-season walima served by three of my old students. Their zealous hospitality was quite overwhelming.

There is something sensual about dipping into a bowl of hot curry, fingers burning at the touch, and nails, dyed yellow with the turmeric, emerging out of the bowl. The taste is not too fiery, the spices are never overbearing and there is a sublime smoothness to the curry. The meal doesn't leave

---

[1] Abaya gowns are loose over-garments or wraps worn by Muslim women when they venture outside their homes. They are often paired with a headscarf. Abayas are taken off when women reach homes or women-only venues.

the guests feeling dyspeptic or too full. In fact, after two to three hours they find themselves almost ready for another meal. The generation before ours often went to the feast with a large tiffin box or a pan to be filled up and taken home. My grandfather would just send a nashteydaan and a salami envelope for the newlyweds if he was unable to attend.

My mother tells me that earlier the curry used to be thinner and golden hued. The word 'taar' denotes the lustrous layer of ghee that covers the gravy. The ghee-laced gravy used to pour like a glistening golden thread (taar) from the spoon. Nowadays, the Rampuris favour a thicker curry brimming with spice-hued, vermilion-red ghee. The parameter now is that the gravy should be easily 'lifted' with the morsel of roti along with a piece of meat. This parameter ensures that the meat pieces are lean and never larger than an inch or two. I'm told that bones and the bone stock were an essential part of the gravy which might have contributed to the sheen of golden taar.

I remember a wedding feast from my childhood: we were seated on durries at a low table that ran the length of the veranda. The curry was served in and eaten from earthen bowls. Whether it was the aroma of asli (pure) ghee used at that time, the tinge of earthiness from the bowls, or the homeliness of the era before marriage halls became impersonal wedding venues, I have never been able to replicate the taste or experience of that taar roti. We laughed hysterically watching a few ladies who were too full to get up from the floor and were being heaved up by helping hands thrust under their armpits!

The curry in taar roti is a 'qaliya', distinct from the familiar 'qorma'. Qaliya, a term not in current usage, is the basic meat curry with turmeric, which might or might not contain vegetables. Qorma is more elaborate and fragrant and has no turmeric. As per the Rampur culinary archives, the technique of making qorma is different from that of qaliya. For qorma, the meat is first mixed with curd, salt and ginger paste; golden-fried onions are added to the meat curry. Further, the use of garlic and powdered almonds distinguishes it from qaliya. At times, piloo biranj (powdered rice) was used in qaliya to thicken the gravy.

Recent articles on Rampur cuisine talk of 'taar qorma' as the signature dish of Rampur. Begum Jahanara Habibullah writes that 'qaliya taar' was a favourite dish of the Rampuris. The common parlance for the dish today in Rampur is 'taar roti' or 'gosht roti'. What we eat in Rampur today, in the garb of taar roti, is not strictly qaliya, but it is not the classic qorma either. I would say that it is an elaborate qaliya which has borrowed some ingredients from qorma and dressed itself up for the occasion.

The food legend goes that the idea of a qaliya, prepared by slow cooking the meat with all the spices, seems to have originated at the time of Muhammad Bin Tughlaq, when he decided to shift his capital from Delhi to Daulatabad in 1327. The enforced mass migration of the army and the populace necessitated a basic meat dish to feed the camp in transit. The Tughlaqs were Turkish, and their cuisine had kababs, meat and vegetable stews and different kinds of bread; the idea of a basic meat dish into which vegetables could be added might have evolved from their eating practices to feed the large populace in transit.

The meat and vegetable combination in Persian cuisine is called 'ghormeh', which might have inspired the preparation of qaliya in Mughal India. Recipes of qaliya with turnips, beets and carrots are described in the original archives of Rampur cookbooks as well as in the collected works from various provincial cultural centres preserved at the Raza library, Rampur. A similar recipe is found in Mughal writing *Nuskha e Shahjahani* and the nineteenth-century *Alwan e Neymat* by Mulla Bulaqi Dehlvi. In both the Delhi and Rampur recipes, the meat is first tempered with ghee and onions; then the vegetables are added and boiled with the meat to obtain a stock. The stock is the base of the curry, which is thickened with rice powder. The general perception of qaliya today is that it is a turmeric-based curry. However, in all the works mentioned earlier, there is no mention of turmeric in the qaliya. The qaliya of yore must have tasted completely different from the qaliya cooked in our homes today. Most of us do not use the term 'qaliya' anymore. We call it 'shorba', which is basically soup or stock, or 'saalan' which denotes curry.

Another variant is the 'chashnidaar qaliya', which is sweet and savoury owing to the sweet syrup added to the curry at the end of cooking. Though the recipe for chashnidaar qaliya is found in cookbooks collected and commissioned at Rampur, there is hardly any evidence that sweet and savoury qaliya was prepared in Rampur. Maybe it was more popular in Awadhi or Mughal cuisine where a mixture of tastes was appreciated, as in Persia. At some point it might have been served at the royal tables that had accommodated the sweet and savoury mutanjan pulao.

Aurangabad has the naan qaliya dish much like the Rampuri taar roti. At an Allahabad wedding, I ate a similar tel gosht preparation cooked in mustard oil, which, I was told, is common in the eastern Uttar Pradesh belt. The general idea remains the same—to feed a large number of people with the least effort. In Rampur, taar roti is also served at funerals, teeja (third) and chaaliswan (fortieth) days of remembrance after the funeral, and at a host of other religious ceremonies involving birth, circumcision and Quran-reading events besides walimas.

Begum Jahanara Habibullah describes the kundan qaliya as one of the prominent dishes served at the Rampur royal dining table. The kundan qaliya, introduced into the Mughal cuisine at the time of Emperor Akbar, is a light, golden-hued mutton gravy with turmeric and saffron as important ingredients. It was called kundan qaliya for its golden curry and had both mutton and chicken meat. It is no longer cooked in Rampur. My husband's aunt is often remembered for her mutton kundan qaliya. According to family culinary memory, she sieved the masalas through a piece of muslin cloth to ensure that the curry was light. The fibrous parts of garlic and ginger would make the curry too thick for a proper kundan qaliya. A similar process is prescribed in Rampur cookbooks.

Shabdegh (shab: night; degh: cooking utensil) is another kind of qaliya, which, whenever prepared, was cooked through the night. The dish was probably imported from Mughal or Awadhi cuisines. Begum Jahanara Habibullah describes it as containing mutton chops and koftas (meatballs) along with turnips studded and filled with jaggery. It seems to have been a delicacy among Rampur elite families. *Shahi Dastarkhwan*, a cookbook written in the 1940s by a Rampur khansama who migrated to Pakistan, says that Rampuri shabdegh was the best in the region. Only the old families remember the shabdegh now, and it has passed into culinary memories of old khansamas. Historically, Rampur was known for its qaliyas.

In some places, ground coconut, cashews or almonds are used to thicken the gravy. The Rampur cooks rarely add coconut powder to the dish as it compromises on the taste and makes the curry sweet, though they have started adding cashew paste now. I wholeheartedly agree. Lazy khansamas are known to use coconut powder to thicken the curry, and it also cuts down the time required for sautéing the masalas. Notwithstanding this, a true gourmand with sensitive taste buds can easily catch the shortcut used by the lazy cook. Some khansamas use powdered melon seeds in sizeable quantities to give a grainy effect to the curry preferred these days.

In my quest to learn the secret of the inimitable curry, I called Munna khansama to cook a 10 kg taar roti at my place for a dinner. Munna khansama cooks unparalleled taar roti in Rampur and is rarely available for small gatherings. Nonetheless, he acquiesced. He specified the type of meat he required and asked us to grind the onions, ginger and garlic; he brought his own aromatic spice mixture. I sat watching him as he lit the wood fire under the massive degh and proceeded to fry chopped onions, casually sipping his tea; he then put in the meat and nearly all the ingredients and sat around smoking and chatting with the servants. I was convinced that it would never turn out to be his famed curry, with such lackadaisical effort. Amazingly, my doubting palate found the same opulent taste in the curry. My non-Rampuri guests went wild with delight, and I packed some taar roti for them to carry home.

Qorma: A Short History of a Long Journey

The qorma is the king of Indian curries. The word 'qorma' has its etymological root in the Turkic 'qavirma'—which denoted a method of frying—and was adapted in Persian, Arabic and Urdu. Turkic 'qavirma' is also the source of the Turkish 'qavurma'. The qavurma (or kavurma) is a fried and braised meat dish found in Turkish cuisine. It is a dry meat dish which sometimes uses preserved meat chunks or mincemeat and is served with pilaf (pulao) or yoghurt. There are several variations of qavurma. 'Sabzi qavurma', or lamb stew with herbs, is a blend of Persian and Turkic cooking; 'Turşu qavurma' combines lamb with preserved lemons and dried apricots and is flavoured with turmeric; while 'Nur qavurma' features lamb and pomegranate. Qovurma, a similar meat stew found in Azerbaijani cuisine, often includes dry fruits, sour grape juice (verjuice) and sometimes vegetables.

Persian cuisine has khoresh, khormeh or ghormeh—a basic stew with vegetables, herbs and kidney beans. The Persian khormeh uses yoghurt and almonds. It has a mild flavour, a thick, creamy texture and base tones of spices and herbs. Across the border, Afghan cuisine has kormeh, a meat curry that gets a slightly sour taste from the use of the limu omani or dried lemons. Incidentally, the use of lemon juice is also advocated in old Rampur cookbooks. It is difficult to trace precise culinary trails of the qorma, which meander and weave through regions and times.

Food historian Neha Vermani writes: 'In the Mughal context, the earliest reference to qorma which I am aware of, comes from aristocratic cookbooks produced during

Shah Alam's reign.'[2] Thus, sometime in the eighteenth century in Mughal kitchens, the meat stew from Persian cuisine assimilated spices, yoghurt, almonds, garlic and other ingredients. This resulted in a thick, spicy curry with fried onions, giving it a classic aroma. Even today, fried and crushed or ground onions with whole spices form the foundational flavour of the Indian qorma. Thus, 'qorma' is named after a style of cooking in which meat is braised over high heat followed by long, slow cooking. In India, the technique of dumpukht—slow-cooking the meat in a dough-sealed pan—is traditionally used to prepare the qorma.

Some food writers claim that a Persian meat curry dish (possibly khormeh) was imbued with Indian masalas through the collaboration of Rajput cooks and Mir Bakrawal, the superintendent of Mughal kitchens. It is sometimes even said that the dish was named after a Rajput clan—Kurma. This origin myth for qorma is highly suspect as no reference to qorma is found in the *Ain i Akbari* or the *Nuskha e Shahjahani* written during the time of Mughal emperors Akbar and Shahjahan respectively. There are, however, a number of qaliya recipes to be found in these accounts. Possibly, the qaliya and do pyaza curries—containing both fried and chopped or ground onions at different stages of cooking—metamorphosed over the years into the Indian qorma in Mughal kitchens making qorma a dish created in the Indian subcontinent.

---

[2] Tarana Husain Khan and Rana Safvi. 'The Real Story of How Qorma Became the King of Indian Curries', *Scroll.in*. Published on 7 November 2020.

It would be safe to assume that by the end of the eighteenth century, the qorma was on the royal menu. The quintessential curry certainly graced the dastarkhwan, the royal table, of the last Mughal emperor, Bahadur Shah Zafar. Munshi Faizuddin Dehlvi, writing with startling detail about the court of Bahadur Shah Zafar in *Bazm e Akhir*, mentions the qorma in the list of dishes at the royal tables. Even before the final disintegration of the Mughal Empire, the qorma was carried to cultural centres of the Indian subcontinent—like Awadh, Hyderabad, Kashmir, Rampur—and amalgamated into the local cuisines.

There are essentially three main variants of the qorma in the subcontinent—the north Indian qorma with yoghurt, almonds, cashews and/or cream; the Kashmiri version that uses fennel seeds, turmeric, tamarind and dried cockscomb flowers; and the south Indian qorma with a pronounced coconut taste. Under the rubric north Indian qorma, there are two styles: Mughlai and Awadhi. According to Lizzie Collingham, the author of *Curry: A Tale of Cooks and Conquerors*, Awadhi cooks added cream to the Mughal qorma and turned it into a sumptuous 'shahi qorma'.

The Nawab of Rampur's kitchen had a specialist khansama, or head cook, who only cooked qorma. A cookbook manuscript, supposedly authored by Nawab Sayed Kalbe Ali Khan (ruled 1865–1887), describes qorma murgh, wherein the meat is marinated in yoghurt and spices (cumin, coriander seeds, cardamoms, cloves, ginger and chillies); onions are fried to golden brown and the marinated meat is added to it along with saffron water. The use of powdered almond and omission of turmeric distinguishes qorma from the qaliya. Rampuri qorma has a distinctive taste—a meaty flavour with few aromatic masalas. It is not a complicated dish to cook, but balancing the flavours and rounding the sharp edges of the spices requires mastery. Most khansamas never reveal their spice mix or the ginger–garlic–onion proportions.

An old khansama revealed the secret of the legendary Rampur qorma to me: add mutton stock from leg bones to the gravy. I tried this technique once—it was tedious, but it changed the dimensions of taste. I would highly recommend using mutton stock for special occasions.

Qorma served with pulao is still the benchmark of culinary skills in Rampur, but the dividing line between qorma and qaliya has blurred. Taar roti, which was originally a qaliya with turmeric, has become faux qorma with the addition of fried onions, the sine qua non of the latter dish. Today, the qorma served at elaborate dinners often has a significant amount of turmeric, which would be considered sacrilege in Mughlai and Awadhi cuisines. Interestingly, the royal and aristocratic families of Rampur do not use turmeric in their qorma, but the practice has become popular across all other social strata. The Rampuris love the vermilion-red colour of the curry and appreciate the sharp flavour of turmeric. Though I prefer the more rounded taste of qorma sans turmeric, I confess to adding a little haldi to jazz things up when I'm in an adventurous mood.

Rampuri Taar Gosht

If Rampuris had to save one dish out of their whole culinary
inheritance, it would undoubtedly be taar gosht.

Ingredients

1 kg mutton
1 cup ghee/refined oil/mustard oil[3]
2 large onions, finely diced
3–4 tbsp onion paste
2 tbsp garlic paste
1 tbsp ginger paste
1 cup yoghurt
2–3 tsp red chilli powder (or as per taste)
2 tsp turmeric powder
5 tsp coriander powder
2 tsp green cardamom powder
10 green cardamoms
7–8 cloves
6–7 bay leaves
1 tsp garam masala powder
1 tsp aromatic masala powder[4]
2 tbsp melon seed powder (optional)
1/2 cup milk

---

[3] The medium of cooking for most of the recipes is ghee, refined oil or
mustard oil. I do not use refined oil for health reasons. However, in several
households, curries and pulaos are cooked in refined oil or vanaspati ghee.
[4] See Cooking Notes.

4–5 drops kewra water[5] (optional)
Salt to taste

Method

1. Heat the oil in a large saucepan or a round-bottomed cooking pot (deghchi). Fry the diced onions till golden. Strain and take out the onions and put them on a large plate. When cool, dry grind them and set aside.
2. In the heated ghee, add the whole cardamoms, cloves and bay leaves.
3. Almost immediately, add the meat, onion paste, ginger-garlic paste, yoghurt and drops of kewra water. Stir to mix everything, and let it cook over a medium flame for 5 minutes.
4. In a bowl, mix turmeric powder, red chilli powder, coriander powder and salt with some water to make a paste. Put this blend into the cooking pot and stir to mix the ingredients. Bring to a boil on a high flame and let it cook for 10 minutes, stirring regularly.
5. Reduce to medium flame and add 2–3 cups of water (depending on the toughness of the meat). Cover and let it cook till the meat is tender. It will take about 30 minutes. A pressure cooker can be used, but the taste of the slow-cooked meat is always better. In case of pressure cooker, use 1 cup of water.
6. Check the meat. If it is tender, add the melon seed powder and the milk. Keep stirring. If the meat is still tough and

---

[5] Screwpine essence or pandanus flower water.

the gravy looks too thick, you can add more water and cook till the meat is tender.

7. When the liquid has nearly evaporated, add the dry-ground fried onion paste. Sauté on a medium flame, adding a splash of water to prevent the curry from burning.

8. When the oil separates from the masala, add boiled water according to the desired consistency of the gravy and bring to a boil. Add the aromatic spice powder, garam masala powder and green cardamom power. Switch off the flame.

9. Taar curry tastes best with tandoor roti.

Rampuri qorma

This is a very old and elaborate recipe of Rampuri qorma. It can be used for mutton or chicken. If chicken is used, remove the meat pieces after frying.

Ingredients

1 kg mutton or chicken
1/2 kg leg bones of goat
1 large cup milk
1/2 cup cream
100 gm almonds
5 gm saffron
4 large onions, finely diced
1 cup ghee or refined oil (you can use 3/4 cup ghee)

3 tbsp onion paste
2 1/2 tbsp garlic paste
2 tbsp ginger paste
1 garlic
1 inch ginger, chopped coarsely
1/2 cup yoghurt
2–3 tsp red chilli powder (or as per taste)
4 tsp coriander powder
2 tsp green cardamom powder
10 green cardamoms
6 cloves
5–6 black cardamoms
6–7 bay leaves
1 tsp garam masala powder
1 tsp aromatic masala powder
4–5 drops kewra water (optional)
Salt to taste

Method

1. Marinate the meat in curd and cream. In a separate bowl, mix the masalas—onion paste, ginger paste, garlic paste, red chilli powder and coriander powder. Set aside. Soak saffron in some milk or kewra (if used). Blanch the almonds and grind to paste.
2. Wash the bones and put in pressure cooker using about 500 ml water. Add 4–5 garlic cloves, chopped ginger, 1 chopped onion and a few bay leaves. Pressure cook till the gelatine and marrow become soft. The stock should be thickish. Add half of the milk and boil for 5 minutes.

Temper with 3 whole cloves and 3 crushed cloves of garlic. If you are in a hurry and need a simpler recipe, you may skip this step. The stock adds an amazing taste to the recipe.

3. In a large pan or pressure cooker, heat the ghee, add the onions and fry till golden. Strain and take out the onions, let them cool, then grind with green and black cardamoms and cloves.

4. Add the marinated meat into the ghee, fry a little and then add the masalas mixed earlier (in step 1). Add bay leaves and let it cook. Keep adding splashes of milk and sauté the meat till the oil separates. If chicken meat is used, first fry the chicken and remove from ghee. Then add the masala mixture and sauté.

5. Add about 500 ml of stock to the curry, keep cooking till meat becomes tender. (Fried chicken can be added back to the curry at this point.) If the meat is not done, boil a cup of water and add. If using a pressure cooker, less water will be required, but the curry comes out better if slow cooked in a pan. (I always cook the chicken in a pan, but some cooks advocate five minutes of pressure-cooking.)

6. When the meat becomes tender, add the fried onion paste and almond paste. Check the consistency of the curry. It needs to be thickish and not too runny. If needed, continue to cook to reduce the water. Add the green cardamon powder, garam masala powder and aromatic powder when it is done.

Qorma Saada

We cook this qorma quite often. It is less elaborate and easy to cook. Recipe by my aunt, Seema Khan.

Ingredients

1/2 kg mutton or chicken[6]
3 medium onions finely diced
3/4 to 1/2 cup ghee or refined oil[7]
1 1/2 tsp garlic paste
1 1/2 tsp ginger paste
2 tsp yoghurt
1–2 tsp red chilli powder (or as per taste)[8]
3 tsp coriander powder
6–7 green cardamoms
5 cloves
2 black cardamoms
1/2 tsp peppercorns
4–5 bay leaves
1/2 tsp garam masala powder
1/2 tsp aromatic masala powder
2–3 drops kewra water (optional)
1 tsp salt or according to taste

---

[6] I have purposely described the measures for 1/2 kg of meat. You will notice that the ingredients for 1 kg meat (in Rampuri qorma) are only slightly more because a certain amount of gravy is required.

[7] The amount of ghee to be used depends on how festive you want the dish to be, or how health conscious you are.

[8] If you have yellow chilli powder, you can use both red and yellow in a 2:1 ratio.

Method

1. In a large pan or pressure cooker, heat the ghee and add half the onions and fry till golden. Drain and grind with whole garam masalas—green and black cardamoms, pepper and cloves. Reserve.

2. Mix curd into the meat with half teaspoon garlic. You can marinate it if you have the time.

3. Mix the ginger–garlic pastes, chilli powder, coriander powder and remaining onions in a bowl.

4. Heat oil. Add meat and sauté on low heat till it changes colour. Add bay leaves and let it cook.

5. Add the mixed masalas. Keep adding splashes of water and sautéing the meat till the oil separates. If cooking with chicken, remove the pieces after frying. Then add the other masalas and sauté.

6. Add about 1/2 litre of water to the curry and keep cooking on medium heat till meat becomes tender. You can add back the chicken here. If the meat is not done, you can boil a cup of water and add. If you are using the pressure cooker, you will need only 3/4 cup of water. I always cook the chicken in a pan, but some cooks advocate a five-minute pressure-cooking.

7. When meat becomes tender, add the fried onion paste. Check the consistency of the curry. It needs to be thickish and not too runny. You can continue to cook to reduce the water. Add the kewra, garam masala powder and aromatic powder when it's done.

Khadey Masaley ka Qorma

This is an elaborate stew distinguished from other qormas in that it doesn't advocate frying onions and braising meat.

Ingredients

1 kg mutton or chicken
1 cup curd
2 tbsp cream (optional)
1 or 3/4 cup ghee or refined oil or mustard oil
4 large onions, roughly diced
2 inch piece of ginger, finely diced
5 dried yellow or red chillies (or as per taste)[9]
3 large garlic bulbs, finely diced
3 tomatoes, roughly diced (optional)[10]
1/2 tsp cumin seeds
10 cloves
20 peppercorns
4 bay leaves
1 1/2 inch piece of cinnamon
1/4 piece of nutmeg
2 pinches of saffron
Salt to taste

Method

1. In a pan or pressure cooker, add the meat with all the masalas, curd, cream and ghee, and cook. If mustard oil is

---

[9] In Rampur, we use yellow chillies instead of dried red chillies for this recipe.
[10] Most Rampuris skip the tomatoes.

used, heat it till the smell evaporates and then add the rest of the ingredients.

2. Add 1/2 cup of hot water if the meat is underdone and keep cooking. Cooking in a pressure cooker might not require extra water.

3. When the meat is tender and the water has evaporated, continue to sauté till the ghee separates visibly. Remove from heat.

4. Garnish with ginger juliennes and serve.

Fish Curry Qaliya

A basic fish curry with a pronounced redolence of fenugreek.
It is more of a casual dish.

Ingredients

1 kg fish (boneless slices of sanwal or mahseer are preferable)
1/2 cup curd
1 tsp fenugreek seeds
1 cup mustard oil
1 large onion diced finely
2 tbsp onion paste
1 tbsp garlic paste
1 tbsp ginger paste
1 tsp turmeric powder
2 tsp coriander powder

1 pinch dried fenugreek leaves (optional)
1-2 tsp red chilli powder (or as per taste)
1 tsp garam masala powder
1 tsp salt (or as per taste)

For washing

200 gm chickpea flour
Juice of 2 lemons
1 tbsp mustard oil

For the garnish

2 tsp chopped coriander leaves
5-6 slit green chillies

Method

1. Wash the fish pieces after rubbing with chickpea flour.
   Then add the lemon juice and/or mustard oil to the
   pieces and wash again.
2. In a flat kadhai, heat the mustard oil till it starts smoking.
   Reduce the flame. Add the fenugreek seeds and let them
   crackle. Add fish pieces in a single layer. Fry them on both
   sides. Be careful not to break the pieces. Drain and remove
   them from the pan and place them in a single layer on a
   dish.
3. Mix the onion paste, ginger-garlic paste, turmeric, chillies
   and coriander powder in a bowl. Now add the mix to
   the oil and sauté. Add curd and keep sautéing till the

oil separates. Keep adding splashes of water so that the masala doesn't burn. The flame should be reduced to prevent burning.

4. Lower the flame and put in the fish pieces carefully in a single layer. Allow to cook for about 10 minutes, turning them over once. The fish pieces become tender after frying. They just need to absorb the masalas.

5. Add slit chillies. Adjust the consistency of curry. If you find it too thick, add 1/2 cup of boiled water. The curry is generally of a thickish texture. Sprinkle a pinch of dried fenugreek leaves if you enjoy the smell of methi.

6. Garnish and serve.

Fish Qorma

This is my grandmother's recipe, and it is the only qorma I remember her cooking. Most of the time, she gave directions and critiques to her khansama and maids. This recipe was contributed by my aunt, Sabiha Khan.

Ingredients

1 kg fish (boneless slices of sanwal or mahseer are preferable)
1/2 cup curd
1 cup mustard oil
2 medium onions, chopped finely
1 1/2 tbsp onion paste

1 tbsp garlic paste
1 tbsp ginger paste
2 tsp coriander powder
1–2 tsp red chilli powder (or as per taste)
1 tsp fenugreek seeds
1 tsp garam masala powder
1 tsp green cardamom powder
1 tsp salt (or as per taste)
10 green cardamoms
3 black cardamoms
6 cloves
10 peppercorns
5 bay leaves

For washing

200 gm chickpea flour
Juice of 2 lemons
1 tbsp mustard oil

Method

1. Wash the fish pieces after rubbing with chickpea flour. Then add the lemon juice and/or mustard oil to the pieces and wash again.
2. Fry the diced onions till golden. Strain and remove them from oil. Grind and add to the curd.
3. In a flat kadhai, heat the ghee or refined oil. For mustard oil, heat it till it starts smoking. Reduce the flame. Add fish pieces in a single layer. Fry them on both sides. Be

careful not to break the pieces. Drain and remove them from the pan and place in a single layer on a dish. Slather the fish pieces with curd and fried onion marinade.

4. Mix the onion paste, ginger–garlic paste, chillies and coriander powder in a bowl.

5. Lower the flame, add fenugreek seeds, cardamoms, cloves and peppercorns and bay leaves in the oil. The seeds should crackle but not get burnt. Now add the above mixture to the oil and sauté. Continue to fry till the oil separates. Keep adding splashes of water so that the masala doesn't burn.

6. Lower the flame and put in the fish pieces carefully in a single layer. Add garam masala powder and green cardamom powder. Allow to cook for about 10 minutes turning them over once. The fish pieces become tender after frying. They just need to absorb the masalas.

7. Add 1/2 cup of hot water if the curry is too thick. Some prefer a thick gravy.

8. Serve hot with roti.

Doodhiya Qorma Murgh or White Chicken Qorma

This is a Rampuri speciality, and it comes out very well. I got this recipe from an old cookbook. It is supposed to be an old Rampuri dish, but I don't remember eating it earlier. My children, Nadir and Rahima, love its simple and elegant flavour.

Ingredients

1 kg chicken (boneless pieces or chicken breasts and legs)
1 or 3/4 cup ghee or refined oil
1 cup milk
1/2 cup cream
3/4 cup curd
10 almonds, blanched and ground
2 tsp white pepper powder (or yellow chilli powder)
1 tsp maida
2 tbsp onion paste
1 tbsp garlic paste
5 green cardamoms
2 black cardamoms
4 cloves
1 tsp garam masala powder
3–4 drops kewra water (optional)
Salt to taste

Method

1. Heat ghee. Add cardamoms and cloves. Fry a bit. Add chicken pieces and fry.
2. Add garlic, almond and onion paste and keep frying till the smell of garlic dissipates.
3. Lower the flame and add curd and cream. Let it simmer till the chicken is almost done.

4. Add milk and maida. Continue to simmer till gravy thickens. Remove from heat, then add white pepper powder and kewra.

5. Serve hot. Sprinkle extra pepper powder if it is too bland. I use yellow chilli powder for extra pungency. But it makes the curry slightly beige rather than white.

White Mutton Qorma

I never had this dish in Rampur, but old-timers often speak of a white qorma. My mother said that their old khansama, Haji Bakka, used to make a similar dish which he didn't teach his successor. I got this recipe from an old khansama. It is simple to cook and turns out to be fabulous.

Ingredients

1 kg mutton
1 or 3/4 cup ghee or refined oil
1/2 cup milk
1 1/2 cup cream
1 cup curd
10 almonds, blanched and ground
3 tsp white pepper powder (or 2 tsp yellow chilli powder if you find it too bland)
1 tsp maida
2 tsp coriander powder

2 tbsp onion paste
1 tbsp garlic paste
6 green cardamoms
4 black cardamoms
4 cloves
1 inch piece of cinnamon
1 tsp garam masala powder
3-4 drops kewra water (optional)
Salt to taste
5-6 slit green chillies, for garnishing

Method

1. Add ground almond, garlic-onion pastes, coriander powder and curd to the meat.
2. Heat ghee or oil. Add cardamoms, cinnamon and cloves. Fry a bit. Add meat and sauté till oil separates.
3. Add 1/2 cup of milk into the cream and make it thin. Add to the meat and keep cooking. Put a tava under the pan so that the masalas don't stick to the bottom of the pan and get burnt.
4. Mix maida in the remaining milk and add to the meat. Continue to cook till meat is tender. You may add more water if the meat is tough. You can also use a pressure cooker.
5. Remove from flame and add salt and pepper and mix well.
6. Serve hot. Garnish with slit green chillies. Sprinkle extra pepper powder if it is too bland.

Pasanda Qaliya

Pasanday (plural) are leg of lamb, or goat fillets cut in thin
slices. It can be made into curries or kababs and was a
popular Mughlai dish. 'Pasanda' means favourite.

Ingredients

1 kg pasanda meat
3/4 cup ghee or oil[11]
1/2 cup milk
1 tbsp hung curd
1/2 tbsp green papaya paste or 1 tsp tenderizer powder
    (optional)[12]
1 medium onion, finely diced
2–3 tbsp onion paste
1 1/2 tsp garlic paste
1 1/2 tsp ginger paste
1–2 tsp red chilli powder
1 tsp yellow chilli powder
2–3 tsp coriander powder
1 tsp turmeric powder
1 tbsp parched gram powder
10 green cardamoms
2 black cardamoms
8 cloves
4–5 bay leaves

---

[11] You may use less, but that is not a good idea. Remove the excess oil later if
    you wish.
[12] Tenderizer depends on the meat.

1 tsp garam masala powder
Salt to taste

Method

1. Fry the onions in ghee till golden. Drain and remove. Grind them with the cardamoms and cloves (except bay leaves) and reserve.
2. Wash and dry the pasandas on a kitchen towel. Take each piece and flatten with a pestle to break the ligaments.
3. In a bowl, mix the curd, tenderizer and garam masala powder. Marinate the pasanda in the mixture for at least an hour.
4. Heat oil. Fry the pasandas on medium flame till they change colour. This will take about 3-4 minutes. Add garlic, ginger and onion pastes and continue frying. Add turmeric, coriander and chilli powder. Add bay leaves and salt.
5. Continue to sauté and add splashes of water till the masala is done and the oil separates. In our kitchen, we mix the ginger-garlic-onion pastes with the powdered spices and put it in all together.
6. Add a cup of water and milk and pressure-cook till the meat is tender. Add gram flour.
7. Stir intermittently till excess water has evaporated. The texture should be thickish with oil on top.
8. Serve hot with pulao or roti.

Kofta Qaliya/Meatball Curry

My mother, who has never made koftas in her life, always judges cooks by their kofta curry, which, she says, is the most difficult dish to prepare. Sometimes Akhtar Bhai, our khansama, who is known for his kofta curry, too, serves us mush because koftas, if not made perfectly, can easily disintegrate. One should judge the tenderness of the meat before adding the tenderizer.
The meat should be fresh and finely minced. Frozen meats often don't come out well.
Koftas are frequently served with kadhi in Rampur.

Ingredients

For the koftas or meatballs

1/2 kg mincemeat, from lean meat
1/2 teaspoon poppy seeds
4 tsp parched gram powder
1 tsp garam masala powder
1/2 tsp aromatic powder
1/2 tsp red or yellow chilli powder
1 tsp ginger paste
1 tsp garlic paste
1 egg (optional)
1/4 tsp green papaya paste or 1/4 tsp tenderizer powder[13] (optional depending on the meat)
1/2 tsp salt or to taste

---

[13] If it is rare and fresh mince, you should not use tenderizer. The best way to check is to fry one meatball in the curry. If it gets hard then add tenderizer to the mince. If the kofta starts falling apart, use some more parched gram powder and egg to bind it. Try again. If all fails, fry the mincemeat as kababs and use the curry for meat!

For the stuffing

1 medium onion, diced into tiny squares
3–4 green chillies, chopped finely
1 bunch coriander leaves, chopped finely

For the curry

3/4 cup (or less) ghee or oil
1 tbsp curd
1 tbsp cream (optional)
1/2 cup milk (optional)
1 medium onion, finely diced
2 tbsp onion paste
1 1/2 tbsp garlic paste
1 1/2 tbsp ginger paste
1–2 tsp red chilli powder (or as per taste)
1 tsp yellow chilli powder
2–3 tsp coriander powder
1/2 tsp turmeric powder
4–5 drops kewra water (optional)
1/2 tsp saffron (optional)
1 tsp garam masala powder
1 tsp aromatic powder
6 green cardamoms
2 black cardamoms
5 cloves
1/2 tsp black peppercorns
4–5 bay leaves
1 tsp salt or to taste

Method

1. Prepare the koftas by thoroughly mixing all the ingredients (except egg and tenderizer). Roughly grind in the mixer-grinder or use a stone mortar and pestle. Set aside.

2. Heat the oil in a large thick-bottomed pan. Fry the onions in it till golden. Drain and remove. Grind onions and reserve. Soak saffron in 1 tablespoon of warm milk.

3. In the same oil add bay leaves. Mix curd, cream, turmeric powder, chilli powder, coriander powder, ginger–garlic–onion pastes and sauté on simmer till oil separates. Add salt. Make sure that the masalas don't burn. Keep adding splashes of water. Useful tip: it's better to put less salt initially because you have added salt in the meatballs as well.

4. Add the fried onion paste and sauté. Add milk, garam masala powder and aromatic powder.

5. Make medium-sized meatballs (about 8–10), stuffing them with onions, green chillies and coriander. If this seems difficult, mix the stuffing into the mincemeat and shape meatballs. The meatballs should be absolutely smooth. Put oil or ghee on the palms when shaping them.

6. Drop one kofta in the curry and test. Let it cook, keep turning it over. Take it out and check. If it is too hard, add tenderizer to the rest of the meat. If it is too soft and is disintegrating, add raw egg to the mincemeat. Put the koftas gently into the curry.

7. Cook on simmer. Shake the pan to turn the koftas every 7–8 minutes till they are done.

8. If the curry is too dry, add about 1/4 cup of water to cook the koftas. The koftas should be brown on the inside, not

pinkish. The curry should neither be too thick nor too runny. Add saffron milk with saffron strands and kewra, if desired.

9. Garnish with chopped coriander leaves. Serve hot.

Nargisi Kofta

Koftas with boiled-egg stuffing are called nargisi after the narcissus flower. When the koftas are cut open, they have a yellow yolk centre surrounded by white, resembling the Nargis flower, hence the name.
Make the koftas and curry exactly as in the above recipe. Do not add tenderizer but ensure that the meat is rare, fresh and minced fine. Hard boil 4 or 5 eggs and shell them. The koftas are made with the boiled egg at the centre coated with the mincemeat stuffing to make the meatballs. Cut koftas lengthwise before serving.

Palak Kofta

I can never live down the day Akhtar Bhai served palak koftas with pureed spinach! It was like having koftas in palak paneer gravy. The spinach should be finely shredded and cooked in the masalas to get the particular texture of palak kofta curry—leafy mush with a halo of vermilion-red oil.

Ingredients

For the koftas/meatballs

1/2 kg mincemeat, from lean meat
1/2 tsp poppy seeds
4 tsp parched gram powder
1 tsp garam masala powder
1/2 tsp aromatic powder
1/2 tsp red or yellow chilli powder
1 tsp ginger paste
1 tsp garlic paste
1 egg (optional)
1/4 tsp green papaya paste or 1/4 tsp tenderizer powder (optional. I prefer not using any tenderizer in this curry.)
Salt to taste

For the stuffing

1 medium onion, diced into tiny squares
3–4 green chillies, chopped finely
1 bunch coriander leaves, chopped finely

For the curry

3/4 cup (or 1/2 cup) ghee or oil
250 gm spinach, washed and chopped finely
1 medium onion finely diced

2 tbsp onion paste
1 1/2 tbsp garlic paste
1 tbsp ginger paste
1-2 tsp red powder (or as per taste)
1 tsp yellow chilli powder
1/2 tsp dried fenugreek leaves or 1 tbsp fresh leaves finely chopped (optional)
1 1/2 tsp coriander powder
1 tsp turmeric powder
1 tsp garam masala powder
Salt to taste

Method

1. Prepare the koftas by thoroughly mixing all the ingredients (except egg and tenderizer). Roughly grind in the mixer-grinder or use a stone mortar and pestle. Set aside.

2. Heat the oil in a large thick-bottomed pan. Fry the onions in it till golden.

3. Mix turmeric powder, chilli powder, coriander powder, ginger-garlic-onion pastes and sauté on simmer till oil separates. Make sure that the masalas don't burn. Add chopped spinach and sauté. Leave on simmer till spinach is cooked and mushy. There should be some water left to cook the meatballs.

4. Make medium-sized meatballs (about 8-10) stuffing them with onions, green chillies and coriander. If this seems difficult, mix the stuffing into the mincemeat and shape meatballs. The meatballs should be absolutely smooth. Put oil or ghee on the palms when shaping them.

5. Drop one kofta in the oil and test. Let it cook and keep turning it over. Take it out and check. If it is too hard, add tenderizer to the rest of the meat. If it is too soft and is disintegrating, add raw egg to the mincemeat. Put the koftas gently into the curry.

6. Cook on simmer in an open pan, shaking the pan to turn the koftas every 7–8 minutes. The koftas should be brown on the inside, not pinkish. The spinach should be tender and mix into the curry. Add methi.

7. Let the excess water evaporate. The texture should be thick.

8. Garnish with chopped coriander and green chillies. Serve hot.

Nahari Curry

This curry is supposed to be slow cooked all night and eaten in the morning (nahaar), but these days we pressure-cook it to speed up the process. Nahari curry tastes best when cooked on a wood-fired chulha through the night. Very often traditional khansamas reserve some curry and ghee from a slow-cooked nahari and use it for preparing the next batch.

Ingredients

For the curry

1 kg mutton or lamb (shank meat cut into large chunks)
1 kg marrow bones

500 gm ghee or 500 ml refined oil
2 large onions, finely diced
1 1/2 tbsp garlic paste
1 tbsp ginger paste
1 tbsp red chilli powder (or as per taste)
1 tbsp deghi mirch
2 tbsp coriander powder
1 tsp turmeric powder
1 tsp garam masala powder
1 tbsp salt or to taste

For thickening

1/2 cup whole wheat flour
1/2 tsp garam masala powder

Special Nahari Masala[14]

1 1/2 tbsp fennel seeds
1/2 tbsp cumin seeds
1 tbsp black pepper
7-8 cloves
1 tbsp coriander seeds (optional)
1/2 tbsp dried ginger (saunth) powder or 1 inch piece of saunth
1/4 nutmeg
2 inch cinnamon piece
2 pieces of mace

---

[14] Dry grind to put into the curry. Remove the veins of the bay leaves.

1 star anise
4 black cardamoms
6–7 bay leaves (small)
5–6 peepli or kababchini

For the garnish

7–8 green chillies, chopped
2 inch ginger, julienned into long, thin pieces
2 bunches coriander leaves, chopped
2 lemons cut into wedges

Method

1. Heat the oil in a large pressure cooker (5 litres or more) or a deghchi. Fry the diced onions till golden. Strain and take out the onions and put them on a large plate. When they cool, reserve half for garnish and dry grind or crush the rest and set aside.
2. In the heated ghee, add the rest of the curry masalas and bones. Sauté on a medium flame, and keep adding splashes of water to prevent the curry from burning.
3. When the oil separates from the masala, add the nahari masala powder, about 1 to 1 1/2 litres of water and bring to a boil. Lower the heat and pressure-cook for 45–50 minutes. If slow-cooking, it will take about 5 hours. You have to add 2 to 3 litres water if you are slow-cooking. Add the meat pieces after the bones are done and cook for about 20 minutes in the pressure cooker. It will take an hour in an open pan. The meat should be well done

and the gelatine in the bones should be soft. Remove the bones and take out the marrow. Put it into the curry. Add half-crushed onions.

4. Dry roast the flour till it slightly changes colour and releases an aroma. It should not become brown. Add garam masala. Mix it into a cup of water and stir making sure that lumps do not form.

5. Tilt the pan and remove the oil on top. Add the flour mixture to the curry to thicken it. Stir and boil for 5 minutes on low heat. You can put a tava under the pan so that the curry doesn't burn.

6. When serving the nahari, add back the ghee removed earlier. Garnish with coriander, green chillies, ginger and the rest of the fried onions and serve hot. Put extra garnish in small bowls along with lemon wedges before serving. It tastes best with khameeri roti.

Paya or Trotter Curry

This is a favourite one-dish winter meal served with khameeri roti.

Ingredients

1 kg mutton or lamb (shank meat cut into large chunks)
1 kg marrow bones and trotter bones (4 trotters serve about 10 people)

For the yakhni stock

2 tsp salt
1 tsp turmeric powder
2 garlic bulbs
2 inch ginger, cut roughly
2–3 cinnamon pieces
10 bay leaves

For the gravy

750 ml to 1 litre refined oil/mustard oil
2 large onions, finely diced and golden fried
3–4 tbsp onion paste
1 1/2 tbsp garlic paste
1 tbsp ginger paste
1 cup curd
2–3 tsp red chilli powder (or as per taste)
1 tbsp deghi mirch (optional, for colour)
5–6 tbsp coriander powder
1 tsp turmeric powder
5–10 green chillies chopped
10 green cardamoms
8 cloves
5–6 black cardamoms
1/2 mace
1/4 nutmeg
6–7 bay leaves
1 tsp garam masala powder
1 tsp aromatic masala powder
Salt to taste

For the garnish

7–8 green chillies, chopped
2 inch ginger, julienned into long, thin pieces
2 bunches coriander leaves, chopped
2 lemons cut into wedges

Method

1. Clean and wash the trotters and bones. If they are not clean enough, blanch in boiling water and throw away the water.
2. Prepare the trotter stock by adding the bones, half measures of the yakhni ingredients and 2–3 cups of water. Pressure cook for about 30–40 minutes till the trotters are done and there is a stickiness to the yakhni water. Remove the bones and sieve the yakhni. Reserve the water.
3. In a pressure cooker, boil the meat with the rest of the yakhni ingredients and 2 cups water till the meat is tender.
4. Remove meat and sieve the yakhni. Add it to the bones yakhni. This water will be added into the curry.
5. Heat oil or ghee in a pressure cooker and golden fry the onions. Drain and remove from oil. Add half the cardamoms, cloves and grind. Set aside.
6. Add the whole spices and bay leaves to the oil. Add all the gravy masalas (except curd and salt) and sauté with the meat till the oil separates. Add curd and 2 cups of water.
7. Add the bones and the fried onion paste. Sauté.
8. Now add the yakhni water according to the consistency of gravy required. Let it simmer. Add salt. A useful tip: check before adding salt since the yakhni is salty. Check

the consistency of the curry; it should be thin but not too
runny.

9. Garnish with coriander, green chillies and ginger, and
   serve hot. Put extra garnish in small bowls along with
   lemon wedges before serving. It tastes best with khameeri
   roti. People also eat paye with plain boiled rice, so it is
   served with plain rice or sometimes with pulao.

Three

The Sense of Rampuri Khichdi

I'm a khichdi-challenged Rampuri, a closet khichdi-hater, and if people come to know about my gastronomic abnormality, it will basically translate to sort of social ostracization in Rampur, the land of urad-khichdi fanatics. I can never comprehend this fascination for the boiled urad dal and rice dish which is a staple winter afternoon diet for Rampur Muslims across all social strata. The non-Muslims are less passionate about it. It is what a sarson saag and makka roti meal is for the Punjabis, although they do not eat it nearly every day throughout winter. Enter any Rampuri home in the old city at lunch time and you'll find a piping hot khichdi lunch in progress with condiments according to means.

My mother is shocked at my strange behaviour and annoyed with me every winter. I think the surprise is less due to intentional amnesia rather than the belief that I will get over this unnatural repugnance. I can only blame it on my non-Rampuri father who ate khichdi reluctantly, saying that

it were the condiments and accompanying dishes that gave it
any taste. Since my father is not around to defend me, I trudge
along with my khichdi-loving Rampuri husband to khichdi
dawats. Yes, khichdi dawats abound throughout winters—a
nightmare for me. Let's say that khichdi in winters has more
social life than pulao. A khichdi dawat has several subtexts
and social layering. It indicates certain amount of closeness,
a bond—a genial mix of informality and hospitality. Close
friends often invite themselves over for khichdi—this is
highly appreciated and indicative of deep kinship. The newly
wed groom, after numerous lavish dinners, finally becomes a
part of the family when he is invited to khichdi at his in-laws'
place. To refuse a khichdi dawat is tantamount to rebuffing
an extended arm of friendship and bonhomie. To confess a
distaste for the dish is social death. Tongue-in-cheek remarks
will echo down generations, and the labels of being too
snobbish and angrez will stick forever. We have welcomed a
few vegetarian daughters-in-law with open arms but a khichdi-
denier is unforgivable. So, khichdi it is throughout winters
within the loving, informal ambit of 'Rampuriyat', with fingers
dipping into mounds of khichdi and glistening with ghee.

In the time of our ancestors, when the notion of
communicable diseases and infections had not marred
social proximity, khichdi was served in a large, round, clay
dish with dollops of ghee buried in its centre. Three or four
people sat around it on the dastarkhwan—a cloth spread on
the floor or bench to serve food in Muslim households—
and ate, with the ghee percolating down the edges of the
dish, frantically mixing chutney, mooli achar, gobhi gosht
before it all turned cold. The bonding effect of eating from

the same plate now exists in the realm of fantastical food stories.

Luckily, when the Rampuris mean a khichdi meal, it includes gobhi gosht, saag kofta, qeema and chicken, along with a host of other condiments—chutney, dahi bada, muli achar, ghee, til oil, etc. So, khichdi is just the base and you add in different combinations of condiments. A chronic conformist, I disguise my gastronomic aberration by taking a tiny spoonful of khichdi and piling it with the curries.

Some Rampuris are so loyal to the dish that they start eating khichdi from late September and gorge on it till April. But the traditional khichdi-eating can only begin when freshly harvested rice and urad dal become available. The new rice is softer and can be cooked with very little water and there is a fresh edge to the new urad dal. But before the khichdi season is declared, the lady of the house must prepare the mooli achar, which consists of boiled radish slices in spicy water, kept in the sun till it matures. The mooli slices and water are also put into the khichdi and the water is gulped down after the khichdi meal for digestion.

Rampuris who are forced to leave this land of winter khichdi complain that the khichdi never tastes the same abroad. I remember that new rice and dal were brought from Rampur every winter at my grandparents' house— the umbilical cord never severed after decades of moving to Aligarh. Some fanatics living outside Rampur even carry water in large plastic jars in the belief that the taste of the khichdi is enhanced by Rampuri water. The urad dal khichdi is only confined to the earlier Rohilla Pathan belt centred around Moradabad, Bareilly and Shahjahanpur. East of

Shahjahanpur, according to Rampuris is, all poorab, the land
of the arhar dal and moong dal khichdi. Moong dal khichdi
(which I prefer) is allowed only in case of an upset stomach.

Till the 1980s, khichdi was cooked only with 'tilak
chandan' rice, a highly aromatic, small grained local variety,
which has become almost extinct now, ousted by the high-
yielding hybrid varieties. Old-timers still lament about the
disappearance of tilak chandan rice and its fabulous aroma,
which announced that khichdi was on boil.

Today, Rampuri khichdi consists of rice and urad dal
boiled with salt, peeli mirch (dried yellow chillies) and slivers
of ginger. It is the simplest dish in itself as no oil or aromatic
spices are ever used. But the proportion of rice and urad dal
as well as the soft, slightly fluffy texture comes with years of
practice.

The khichdi used to have elaborate versions too, as I found
in my translation of the manuscripts of Persian cookbooks.
There used to be a 'khichdi pulao', which had meat cooked
with spices—to make a yakhni stock—and married to the
moong dal khichdi. Similarly, recipes of dhuli khichdi and
muqasshar khichdi have moong pulses, rice and meat, cooked
with ghee and spices. Gujarati khichdi and bhuni khichdi
were the non-meat khichdis, and dated back to the Mughal
era. The most interesting recipe is of khichdi Daud Khani,
possibly named after the founder of Rohilkhand or a Mughal
nobleman; it consists of moong pulses, rice, mincemeat,
spinach and eggs—a complete meal for a warrior! Interestingly,
most of the khichdi recipes use moong lentils and rice as
the base, but the quintessential Rampur khichdi uses urad
lentils, maybe because urad is more commonly grown in the

area. There is no mention of urad dal khichdi, which we call Rampuri khichdi in the Raza Library manuscripts. Probably, the humble urad dal khichdi was too simple to be included in the cookbook manuscripts which drew inspiration from the grand Mughal and Awadhi cuisines. However, oral history is replete with instances of the Nawabs of Rampur relishing the urad dal khichdi.

My grandfather-in-law, Ameer Ahmad Khan, riyasat engineer and chief secretary to Nawab Sayed Raza Ali Khan (ruled 1930–1949), was sometimes called for a khichdi meal at 3 a.m. The Nawabs stayed up all night entertained by music and dance mehfils. Urad khichdi was a great favourite of Rampur Nawabs who enjoyed both the royal as well as the plebeian cuisine.

An interesting account of Nawab Sayed Hamid Ali Khan is narrated by Sayed Muhammad Yameen in *Urdu Digest* (February 1968), which he heard from his father-in-law, Colonel Sayed Ahmad Hashmi, when he was posted at the Nawab's court. The story goes that Nawab Sayed Hamid Ali Khan was eating biryani one day, and he found a piece of bone in the rice. A jamadar used to be present at the meal with a whip, and a maulvi recited the 'bismillah' incantation at every morsel the Nawab raised to his royal lips. The biryani cook was summoned and whipped for his carelessness. On another day, the Nawab was partaking of his favourite urad dal khichdi. He happened to appreciate the dish and called the cook to reward him. It was the same cook who had been whipped for his biryani. The cook said, 'Huzoor, my father was the biryani cook at your grandfather Nawab Sayed Kalbe Ali Khan's court. Once he cooked khichdi for Sir Sayed Ahmad

Khan, founder of Aligarh Muslim University, who was a state guest. The Nawab was pleased and wanted to reward him, so my father requested that, of his four sons, he wanted three of them to be educated at Aligarh Muslim University and their education be sponsored by the Rampur State. So, while my brothers went to the University, I stayed back to learn my father's skills and serve Your Highness. Now, I have four sons and I request Your Highness to give me the same reward for my khichdi.'

After confirming the story, the Nawab sent the cook's three sons to Aligarh Muslim University. In Rampur, fortunes can change with a well-cooked khichdi.

My writings on Rampur cuisine and tilak chandan rice evoked the interest of historian Professor Siobhan Lambert-Hurley from the University of Sheffield. As we connected over Skype calls, Professor Lambert-Hurley and Professor Duncan Cameron—plant scientist at the Institute of Sustainable Food, University of Sheffield—put together a project for resurrection of tilak chandan and revival of heritage recipes. 'Forgotten Food: Culinary Memory, Local Heritage and Lost Agricultural Varieties in India'—funded by the Arts & Humanities Research Council in the United Kingdom and executed under the lead of University of Sheffield—was born in November 2019. An integral part of the project was growing tilak chandan in Rampur and attempting to resurrect it by making the plants disease resistant through plant biology interventions in special plant labs at Sheffield. After a frantic search for tilak chandan seeds in the middle of the pandemic, we were able to locate the elusive seed, get its authenticity confirmed by Professor Cameron and grow it at the historic

Benazir farms in the shadow of the ruins of Benazir palace of the Rampur Nawabs. In December 2020 after several twists and turns, which included a freak storm a few days before the harvest, we were able to reap the almost mythical tilak chandan.

I organized a khichdi dawat for my friends—a sort of taste test for the newly harvested tilak chandan. This was a part of the blind test we had planned under the project. As the khichdi simmered, I caught a whiff of something forgotten, an aroma of my childhood and youth. Since it was new rice, it tended to become lumpy even when cooked with little water. Old-timers say that the traditional Rampur khichdi made from new rice and new lentils was supposed to be soft and kind of sticky in texture. No wonder my mother prefers a slightly overcooked khichdi. Tilak chandan is a smaller and plumper grain than the hybrids we had become used to, and when I served the khichdi with spoonfuls of clarified butter, each grain was completely coated in a way that long grained hybrid rice could not aspire to. To make things exciting, I also cooked khichdi with long grained basmati rice. The texture of basmati rice khichdi was fluffy but had no aroma. My eight unsuspecting friends were all in their forties and fifties, had lived in Rampur for years and had been exposed to tilak chandan khichdi till the 1990s. One couple had continued to grow tilak at their farms. I served the basmati khichdi first and then the tilak khichdi and was gratified to note that everyone turned to the tilak khichdi as they were jolted out of their taste amnesia. They gushed over the aroma, abandoned their forks to mix ghee with their hands, savouring every bite. My one non-Rampuri friend, who had been married into Rampur, however, preferred the basmati khichdi for its texture. Seduced by that ricey tilak chandan aroma, I almost got over my khichdi-hate.

Khichdi: An Eternal Love Story

Bisma Tirmizi writes in *Feast: With a Taste of Amir Khusro* that khichdi belonged to the soil of the subcontinent and the conquerors over the ages fell in love with the dish. The word 'khichdi' has Sanskrit roots, and the Greek king Seleucus I Nicator during his campaign in India (305–303 BC), wrote that pulses cooked with rice is a popular dish among people of the Indian subcontinent. Ibn Batuta wrote in his account of India (1340), 'The munj (moong) is boiled with rice, and then buttered and eaten. This is what they call "Kishri" and on this dish they breakfast every day.'[1] Raaz Yazdani, poet and historian from Rampur, writes that when Nadir Shah invaded India in the eighteenth century and saw Indians eating pulses, rice and roti together, he is said to have remarked with surprise,

Een hindaan ghalla ra ba ghalla mee khurinda

(These Hindi people mix grains with grains and eat).[2]

Pulses were a novelty to the Muslim conquerors as indeed was khichdi. The Mughals used several aromatic spices and

---

[1] Rev. Samuel Lee. Trans. and ed., *The Travels of Ibn Battuta in Near East, Asia and Africa 1325–1354*. New York: Dover Publication, Inc., 2004.

[2] Raaz Yazdani, *Naya Daur* (Urdu magazine). Published on 26 January 1960.

khichdi became a great favourite with them. They granted them grand names like Khichdi Shahjahani, Khichdi Mahabatkhani, etc.—names which were transcribed into cookbooks and carried on for posterity. It is said that Mahabat Khan, a Mughal noble, ate only one meal a day and millet-rice khichdi was always a part of the repast. One reason for the metamorphosis of this humble peasant fare to high cuisine was the ritual abstinence from consuming meat practised by the Mughal Emperors from the time of Emperor Akbar. Akbar ate khichdi on his meat-abstinence days and it finds mention in *Ain i Akbari*. It was a favourite preparation of Emperor Jahangir; Aurangzeb craved for chickpeas khichdi during his campaign in the Deccan; he also ate a variation of khichdi called the Alamgiri khichdi which had boiled eggs and fish. The British and the Anglo-Indians reinvented khichdi into 'kedgeree' cooked with fresh fish for breakfast.[3] But the unpretentious khichdi survives in its simplest and from-the-heart form in Rampur—a late breakfast meal for the male members before they leave for work, or a lazy lunch before siesta in the sun.

Because of its simplicity, khichdi should be the perfect dish for funerals, right? Bisma Tirmizi describes khichdi served to the mourners after a funeral.[4] However, in Rampur, khichdi is never served at funerals because there are so many condiments that must accompany it that it would be a strain on the mourners. So, pulao comforts the bereaved while khichdi continues to be the dish for leisurely celebration of winter.

---

[3] Lizzie Collingham, *Curry: A Tale of Cooks and Conquerors*. London: Vintage Books, 2006.

[4] Bisma Tirmizi, *Feast: With a Taste of Amir Khusro*. New Delhi: Rupa Publications, 2017.

During Ramzan, the wake-up call for sehri—the meal consumed before dawn by the fasting Muslims—begins at 2 a.m. on the loudspeakers. It is a bit early. The maulvi often calls out, 'Hazraat, it's time for sehri. Start cooking your khichdi.' The shaukeen (foodies) have khichdi even for summer fasts, although people say that it makes you very thirsty.

Once, I found senior students of my class enjoying a khichdi repast during the lunch break, with khichdi brought in casseroles complete with condiments and gobhi gosht. That was one khichdi invite I could refuse because of my exalted position of a teacher.

Urad Dal Khichdi

Ingredients

1 cup rice
1/2 cup black split urad dal
2 inch ginger, shredded into small pieces
5-6 dried red or yellow chillies, broken into half-inch pieces
Salt to taste

Method

1. Wash and clean rice and lentils. Mix together.
2. Add ginger, chillies and salt. Add water. A simple measure to check the quantity of water is that it should stand about an inch over the rice.

3. Cook till rice and lentils are done.
4. Serve hot.

Gobhi Gosht

A simple meat and vegetables dish served with khichdi or a dish that can stand on its own. We never use garam masalas in this.

Ingredients

1/2 kg mutton
1/2 kg cauliflower
1 bunch of spinach, shredded finely
1/2 cup mustard oil
3 medium onions, cut lengthwise
1 tbsp garlic paste
1/2 tbsp ginger paste
1 tsp turmeric powder
1 tsp coriander powder
1-2 tsp red or yellow chilli powder
Salt to taste

For the garnish

2 tsp chopped coriander leaves
5-6 slit green chillies

Method 1

1. Wash and cut the cauliflower into small pieces discarding the base. Wash and cut the spinach. Mix the vegetables.
2. Heat oil till it starts smoking. Reduce flame and fry half the onions till they are golden. Add the meat and fry.
3. Add all the spices to the meat. Put in the cauliflower and spinach and mix well.
4. Pour half a cup of water and pressure cook on high heat till the meat is done. If cooking in a pan, use two cups of water.
5. Open the cooker and cook till all the water evaporates. Keep stirring till the cauliflower and spinach are completely mixed and the curry is a thick mush and the meat pieces are tender but firm. It can also be cooked without spinach, if so desired.
6. Garnish and serve hot.

Method 2

This is a quick recipe and comes out well.

1. Put the meat with all the masalas, vegetables and oil. You don't need to smoke the oil.
2. Add water and pressure cook till meat is done.
3. Open the cooker and cook till all the water evaporates. As in the earlier recipe, the curry should be thick and homogenous. It can also be cooked without spinach, if so desired.
4. Garnish and serve hot.

Mooli Pani ka Achar/Radish Water Preserve

As mentioned earlier, this preserve is a necessary accompaniment to khichdi. It is prepared with fresh winter radishes.

Ingredients

1.2 kg thick radish (without leaves)
2 tbsp rai (mustard seeds)
8–10 dried red chillies (or as per taste)
40–45 garlic cloves
Salt to taste

Method

1. Wash the radish. Peel and slice into thin (about 1/2 cm) round slices.
2. Put in a pan. Add enough water to cover the slices, so that it stands 1–2 inches above them. Add salt.
3. Boil till the slices are tender. Let the radish and water cool.
4. Meanwhile, grind the red chillies, garlic and mustard seeds. Use the boiled water from the radish. It is preferable to grind on the sil-batta the old way. The texture should be coarse and grainy.

5. When the radish and water are cool enough, add the paste. Check if the salt is fine.
6. If there are not enough chillies, add more after grinding them. All the ingredients should be as per taste.
7. Put it into clean jars and let it dry in the sun.
8. Keep in the sun for a few days till it matures and the tangy taste of the rai becomes pronounced. This preserve should be consumed quickly and is not to be kept for long.

Four

Kababs and Forgiving

A couplet by Bahadur Shah Zafar ripped apart the deep familial ties between the two families. Rahat Khan stood looking at his dear friend and mentor. A gentle hand had removed the shroud from the beloved face for the last look—the deedan. He sighed and said:

> Woh jo bechtey they dawa e dil, woh dukaan apni badha gayey[1]

(He who sold medicine to assuage my wounded heart has closed shop.)

Chhunnu Khan bristled, his face reddened with righteous anger. Was this the occasion to spout poetry? Shouldn't the old libertine, known for squandering wealth on musicians and dancers, utter the acceptable Quranic lines of condolence?

---

[1] Bahadur Shah Zafar

'Rahat Khan, please leave!' Chhunnu Khan was not the one to hold back his rage. The grieving patriarch was led away and denied the opportunity to even attend the funeral prayer. Chhunnu Khan seethed, narrated the incident to everyone and awaited an apology that never came. It was beneath Rahat Khan to apologize to a younger brother-in-law and pander to one who lacked the poetic sensibility to comprehend the apt lines. 'I will recite a whole ghazal at his funeral!' thundered Chhunnu Khan.

From then on, the brothers-in-law would turn away from each other if they met by a chance encounter while walking down the common gully, studiously avoiding each other through many Eids, weddings and funerals. The women, first cousins and milk sisters, initially tried to breach the impasse, then ignored the stupid quarrel and continued to visit each other. The estrangement was at first remarked upon by relatives and acquaintances; then it became the expected behaviour. Rampur had several stories of legendary quarrels between close relatives lasting for generations. This was one more family story.

What was torn asunder by poetry was bridged by kababs. Khala Sahab, Rahat Khan's late mother-in-law, had started a tradition of sending a nashteydaan on the eleventh day of every lunar month to Chhunnu Sahab. A large tiffin carrier filled with her renowned bhapi kababs and parathas, a rice preparation and a sweet dish would make its way to Chhunnu Khan's house. This practice was continued even after Khala Sahab's demise by her daughter, Parveen. A servant was sent in the morning to announce the meal. Chhunnu Khan, a fervent Rampuri foodie, eagerly awaited the nashteydaan despite the 'till death overcomes us' estrangement.

'There is no war with food. Allah intensely dislikes dishonouring food,' he would say to his wife. He enjoyed the meal and sent his thanks to his sister-in-law. It was foolish to pass the delectable kababs cooked with the secret family recipe.

Bhapi kababs (steamed kababs), sometimes also called pateeli kababs in Rampur, would arrive in the early evening— round globules standing with poised dignity in an inch of aromatic ghee. They were pale, never crispy browned, like the regular kabab patties, since they were steamed in ghee and their own juices rather than deep fried. Parveen Apa used to prepare the meat in the manner of seekh kababs and they had the same melting succulence, understated spices, the light charcoal barbecue smell ingeniously wrought by smoking the batter with a piece of burning charcoal doused in ghee right before shaping the kababs into large spheroids.

Since a kababi, the elusive seekh kabab cook, is much in demand, expensive and pre-booked for grand feasts, the bhapi kababs are a delicious alternative. Ghee, made aromatic by frying onions and spices, forms the base for slow cooking the bhapi kababs. The mincemeat used for making the kababs is first softened using raw-papaya milk and ginger. The skilled cook must assess the nature and future behaviour of the mincemeat—which itself is prepared from lean meat—and then commit the correct amount of papaya milk. Too much and the kababs would become mush; too little and they would bounce off the walls! Then, fried and ground onions with spices and ground chanas (parched gram) are added to the mincemeat that is ground on the stone sil-batta to make it soft, taking care to remove tendons and scraps, which tend to harden making the kababs too tough. A hand-worked meat grinder screwed on to a wooden bench used to be an essential part of old Rampuri households. Since the task required some technical expertise and muscle power, thought to be lacking in the female species, it was assigned to a male servant. Supervised by the cook, the boy, seated on the bench, would work on the meat grinder, mincing the meat and removing the scraps. Some khansamas and gourmands shun all machines for preparation of mince for kababs and koftas, preferring to work on the meat with a sil-batta. It is a tough job; I confess to using my meat grinder.

The prepared meat is smoked with a chunk of burning charcoal, placed into a hollowed centre on a piece of onion skin. Melted ghee is poured on the glowing charcoal and the vessel is tightly covered with a lid for some time to let the smoky redolence and the flavours settle in. Finally, the prepared mince is shaped into perfect round orbs and put into a narrow-mouthed vessel containing warmed ghee, covered and slow-cooked, and turned intermittently till they are done. The meat juices and the ghee produce the steam. Very often the cooks or the lady of the house reject the meat for they are staking their reputation on the judgement of the critical, expectant gourmets. It's because of the stringent meat requirements and the tedious preparation that bhapi kababs have become an endangered species of the kabab genus. The Awadhi cuisine has a similar style of kababs called the gola kababs.

Bhapi kababs came to my rescue when my mother-in-law's close relatives visited us in Allahabad. I had carried some Rampuri recipes learned from Parveen Apa, the culinary goddess of the family, to Allahabad. Reputations are carved in stone at such dinners. The bhapi kababs cooked to perfection, earned me a culinary standing I still bask in after more than twenty years. Let us say that their low expectations from a not-brought-up-in-Rampur daughter-in-law enhanced the effect.

Only the formidable champions of Rampur cuisine know how to make seekh kababs at home. Lesser mortals like me depend on Kallu Kababi's son to cater to us. We have to book an appointment and he comes home with his iron skewers. Special lean meat from the butchers, coal and raw papaya have to be procured beforehand. The meat must be ground at the grinding machines since we no longer have the trusty hand grinder. Kallu's son (whom we call Kallu for some reason, and he likes it) is an exact replica of his father—gaunt, dark, with curly black locks in disarray. Kallu was a rickshaw-puller who lived near my husband's, Qamar's, ancestral home. My late mother-in-law, a talented gourmet, taught him to make seekh kababs and encouraged him to change his profession because he was too weak to earn a decent living pulling rickshaws. He became famous as Kallu Kababi in the old city area and made a good living till he went blind from the coal smoke. Even then he could feel the texture of the meat and add the right masalas to produce the most delectable Rampuri kababs. His son started assisting him with the hot skewers and has his father's unerring touch. Kababs have the power to change lives—in good, bad and unforeseen ways—and a good kababi is much in demand throughout the year.

Only an experienced kababi can judge the mizaj (temperament) of the meat and put in papaya milk accordingly. Too much tenderizer would reduce the mince to a sloppy pulp and turn kababs into the less preferred (in Rampur) Kakori

kababs or, worse, make them fall off the skewers. The Rampuri
seekh kababs differ from the Lucknowi and Kakori varieties.
They are much thicker and smoother and are golden brown
with dark spots. We use just the minimal garam masalas, so even
the inside of the kabab is beige in colour. Rampuris belittle the
too dark brown, thin and mushy Kakori kababs of Lucknow.

Kallu Kababi used very basic masalas, and so does his
son. He fries the onion rings till they are golden brown and
adds cardamoms, cloves, pepper, some aromatics and grinds
them together. He judges the meat, cuts thick slices of raw
papayas and places them on the meat. Papaya milk is the best
tenderizer and gives a lovely aroma. He is particularly skilled in
judging the exact amount of milk required. He then adds the
fried onion paste, ginger–garlic paste, yellow chillies and some
parched gram powder and kneads them with the mincemeat,
and that's it. The kababs are then slow roasted on the skewers
over coal fire till they turn golden with dark brown spots; they
slide off the skewers for a deep soak in asli ghee to give a
buttery flavour. Some khansamas put the ghee on burning
coals and cover the pan because the low heat helps the flavour
of masalas and ghee settle into the kababs. Sometimes, I avoid
the ghee dunking, but it affects the taste. Anyway, ghee is no
longer the enemy now. I get big batches cooked at home and
deep-freeze them. Recently, some restaurants in Rampur have
started making excellent seekh kababs, but I still prefer the
homemade ones because they taste much better, fall cheaper
and you can be sure of the meat. I have heard that the Lucknow
kababs have a fine balance of thirty types of spices, and the
cook won't hear of making kababs without the kabab chini
spice, which is unheard of among Rampur kababis. I have

included the Kallu-Kababi recipe in my culinary repertoire but if the mincemeat gets too mushy, one can salvage the kababs by just rolling the meat into balls and cooking them as bhapi kababs.

An easier and more common version of kachhey gosht kababs (a raw-meat variety of kababs) are the chapli kababs. They are typical of the Pakhtun (Pathan) cuisine popular in the north Indian Rohilla belt, which includes Rampur. It is an original Pakhtun dish with tribal roots, carried to India by the Rohillas and is still prepared in Peshawar and Afghanistan–Pakistan highlands. Hardy and rustic, the chapli kababs are flat, irregular palm-sized kababs with basic spices, fried onions, chickpea flour and strong garlic overtones. Finely cut onions, green chillies and coriander leaves are kneaded into the mincemeat before deep frying the thin disks. The yellow chilli chutney is the perfect accompaniment for these kababs. Mint and green chilli chutney is used in summers and coriander chutney in winters. Chapli kababs turn out tougher than the melting Lucknow galauti kababs. The average Rampuri disdains the squashy, soft, over-spiced galauti kababs, preferring the no-frills, straightforward chapli kababs. Afghani chapli kababs use coriander seeds and are very large patties—quarter-plate sized or even larger—fried individually. They are served with lamb-meat pulao. Some Rampuri cooks use crushed coriander seeds too; I prefer kababs without the seeds. The Peshawari chapli kababs have raw tomatoes kneaded into the mincemeat which would be considered a gastronomic blasphemy in Rampur.

Shami kababs are my go-to dish if the mincemeat isn't very lean. For all the other kababs, only lean meat will do. The origins of shami kababs remains a culinary debate. They are believed to have been created in the Mughal kitchens, though the name indicates that they are originally from Bilad al Sham (Syria), or were introduced by Syrian cooks. Lizzy Collingham in *Curry: A Tale of Cooks and Conquerors* quotes the oral history that shami kababs were an innovation to cater to Nawab Asif ud Daulah of Lucknow who had lost all his teeth but not his craving for kababs. Some writers quote the same story for galauti kababs.

Meat boiled with chana dal, spices, ginger and garlic forms the base for shami kababs. The meat is then ground and kneaded with finely cut onions, coriander leaves and green chillies. The batter, with a dough like consistency, is shaped into flat, biscuit-shaped discs and deep fried or shallow fried till crisp. Nineteenth century manuscript cookbooks preserved in the Rampur Raza Library advocate sautéing the mince with fried onions, rather than boiling. The other ingredients are roughly the same as the ones used in our usual shami kababs, but a sizeable amount of curd and cottage cheese was added to the batter, which is not used anymore. Finally, the meat is ground and kababs are fashioned. In Maulvi Nazir's bestselling novel *Mirat ul Uroos*—translated as *The Brides Mirror* and published in 1899—the heroine instructs the maid to get curd from the market to add to the kabab mincemeat. Apparently, curd used to be an essential ingredient for kababs, possibly to make them softer and reduce the meat odour. I tried cooking these old-style kababs and they turned out quite distinct from our usual shami kababs and were closer to the raw-meat kababs in flavour. My husband missed the crispness of our usual shami kababs, which can only be brought on by boiling the meat with chana dal.

Jahanara Begum, in her memoir, *Remembrance of Days Past*, describes the fish kababs called kabab uroos e behri. Several kilos of sanwal fish were used to make the kabab in the shape of a fish about two feet in length. The scales were fashioned in a way that made the dish look like a whole fish was served on a silver tray. The scales were of a different flavour to the meat inside. It even had a fake tongue of a distinct flavour. This innovative presentation style, learned from the Awadhi khansamas, is all but forgotten in Rampur.

Rahat Khan passed away after a long illness; all the relatives were by his bedside, except Chhunnu Khan. Perhaps, Chhunnu Khan secretly waited for someone to persuade him to give up the long-ongoing standoff. The ladies, as usual, ignored his affectation of unconcern. He, however, attended the funeral prayer with an aura of high-minded dignity, uttering the appropriate Quranic lines of condolence and praying for the departed soul. The nashteydaan bearing bhapi kababs has long since passed into collective food memory and the quarrel into family trivia that evokes nostalgic laughter.

Parveen Apa's Bhapi Kababs

A speciality of Rampur, bhapi kababs bridged the legendary quarrel between two families. These are a bit tricky to cook, for if the meat is not lean or tender, they might turn out to be too tough.

Ingredients

1 kg fine mince of lean meat
1 1/2–2 cups ghee
1 or 1/2 tbsp green papaya paste or 1 tsp tenderizer powder
50 gm parched gram, shelled and powdered
1 large onion, finely diced
1 tbsp ginger paste
1–2 tsp red or yellow chilli powder
10 green cardamoms
3 black cardamoms
6–7 cloves
1 tsp peppercorns
4–5 bay leaves
1 tsp garam masala powder
1 tsp aromatic powder
1 egg (if required)
Salt to taste

Method[2]

1. Fry the onions in ghee till golden. Drain and remove them. Grind them with the garam masalas (cardamoms, cloves and peppercorns, except bay leaves) and reserve.

---

[2] The same method is used for seekh kababs. The mixture is put on skewers and roasted over coals. It requires some skill and expertise. The kababs are dipped in ghee after they are taken off the skewer.

2. Take the mincemeat in a large bowl and add chilli powder (in Rampur we use yellow chillies), aromatic powder, garam masala powder, parched gram powder, papaya paste and salt. Knead them well. Tip: grind the mincemeat in a mixer-grinder or on sil-batta if it appears too rough.

3. Add the fried onions and garam masala paste. Mix thoroughly.

4. Heat oil in a large, thick-bottomed pan and add bay leaves. Lower the flame. Shape the mincemeat into medium-sized balls and put them into the ghee. Turn them once when one side becomes light brown. Tip: first fry one meat ball. If it starts to fall apart, add an egg to the rest of the batter. You can also add breadcrumbs. If the meatball is too hard, you can try to make the mince softer by adding half a teaspoon of tenderizer. If nothing works, shape into flat patties and shallow fry over low heat to make kabab patties.

5. Cover the pan and cook the dish on very low heat, shaking the pan intermittently to turn the kababs. Tip: put a tava (skillet) under the pan if it doesn't have a thick base. The kababs will cook in the steam of their own juices.

6. When all the water evaporates and only the ghee is visible, switch off the flame.

7. Serve it hot with roti or parathas.

Rampuri Murgh Seekh Kabab

A recipe from the old khansamas. It tastes better than our average barbecued chicken. It can also be baked in an oven or cooked in a thick bottomed pan on low heat.

Ingredients

1 kg whole chicken (dressed and skinned) or chicken breast and leg pieces
1 cup hung curd
250 gm paneer (optional)
1 tbsp green papaya paste or 1 tsp tenderizer powder
1/2 cup ghee
1 large onion, finely diced
1 tsp ginger paste
1 tsp garlic paste
1–2 tsp red or yellow chilli powder (or as per taste)
6 cloves
6–7 green cardamoms
3 black cardamoms
1 tsp cumin seeds
1/6 piece of nutmeg
1/4 piece of mace
1 tbsp parched gram powder
1 tsp saffron
1/2 tsp kewra water (optional)
Salt to taste

Method

1. Clean out the whole chicken and wash it thoroughly and dry on a kitchen towel. If using chicken pieces, wash thoroughly and dry on a kitchen towel.

2. Soak the saffron in kewra water or in one tablespoon of warm milk.

3. Fry the onions till golden. Drain and remove. Grind cloves, cardamom, cumin and nutmeg. Add the fried onion to this masala and make it into a paste. Reserve the ghee for basting.

4. Make deep gashes all over the chicken and rub papaya paste and salt on it.

5. In a bowl, mix hung curd, mashed paneer, garlic-ginger-fried onion pastes, gram powder and chilli powder (in Rampur we use yellow chillies). Slather all over the chicken, and fill the cavity of the chicken with the remaining mixture. Tie up the whole chicken with string.

6. Pour saffron water over the chicken. Marinate overnight in the refrigerator or at least for four hours.

7. Put the chicken or chicken pieces on seekh (skewers) and barbecue over charcoals. Rotate the skewers and apply ghee till the chicken is done.

8. It can also be cooked in an oven or a large pan. First, smoke the chicken. Take a large burning piece of charcoal, put it on onion skin or a piece of roti. Put it on the chicken and pour ghee over it. Close the lid tightly for 5 minutes. This will impart the smoky barbecue taste.

Murgh Musallam

This is also an old recipe of the Rampur khansamas, and it comes out really well. The marinade is prepared in the same way as murgh seekh kababs. Some khansamas use boiled eggs for stuffing the chicken.

Ingredients

1 kg whole chicken dressed and skinned
1 cup hung curd
250 gm paneer (optional)
1 tbsp green papaya paste or 1 tsp tenderizer powder
1/2 cup ghee
1 large onion, finely diced
1 tsp ginger paste
1 tsp garlic paste
1–2 tsp red or yellow chilli powder (or as per taste)
6 cloves
6–7 green cardamoms
3 black cardamoms
1 tsp cumin seeds
1/4 piece of nutmeg
1/4 piece of mace
1 tbsp parched gram powder
1 tsp saffron
1/2 tsp kewra water (optional)
Salt to taste

For the stuffing

150 gm mincemeat
2 tbsp oil or ghee
1 medium-sized onion, chopped
1/2 tsp red chilli powder
1 tsp garam masala powder
3–4 green chillies
Salt to taste

Method

1. Clean out the whole chicken and wash it thoroughly and dry on a kitchen towel. Marinate the same way as murgh seekh kabab (above).
2. For the stuffing, heat the oil and fry the onions till golden. Add the mincemeat, chilli powder and green chillies. Keep frying till it changes colour. Add salt and 1/2 cup of water. Put it on simmer till the mincemeat becomes tender. Let the excess water evaporate; set it aside to cool completely.
3. Take out the marinated chicken and fill in the stuffing. Seal the chicken's cavity using toothpicks. Tie the chicken securely with a string making sure that the legs are strung together.
4. In a thick-bottomed pan, heat the ghee and put in the chicken. Fry on both sides on medium heat. Use the leftover ghee to baste the chicken intermittently.
5. Cover the pan and simmer till the chicken is done.
6. Remove the string and serve hot.

Pasanday Kabab Pateeli

Pasanday are thin leg slices or fillets of lamb or goat and were
a popular Mughlai dish.
It can be made into curry or kababs.

Ingredients

1 kg pasanday fillets
1/2 cup of ghee/refined oil/mustard oil
1 cup milk
1 tbsp hung curd
2 tbsp cream
1 tsp green papaya paste or 1 tsp tenderizer powder (optional,
depending on the meat)
1 large onion, finely diced
1 1/2 tbsp garlic paste
1 1/2 tbsp ginger paste
1–2 tsp red or yellow chilli powder
2 tsp coriander powder
1 tsp parched gram powder
1 tsp saffron
10 green cardamoms
2 black cardamoms
1/2 tsp cumin seeds
10 cloves
4–5 bay leaves
1 tsp garam masala powder
1 tsp aromatic powder
4–5 drops kewra water
Salt to taste

Method

1. Fry the onions in ghee till they turn golden. Drain and remove them. Grind the fried onions with the garam masalas (cardamoms, cloves and cumin, except bay leaves) and reserve. Soak the saffron in a little warm milk.

2. Wash and dry the pasanday on a kitchen towel. Take each individual piece and flatten with a pestle to break the ligaments. You have to beat them down.

3. In a bowl, mix the curd, cream, coriander, red chillies (in Rampur we use yellow chillies), kewra, parched gram powder, salt, ginger–garlic pastes, tenderizer, garam masala powder and aromatic powder. Marinate the pasanda in the mixture for at least 1–2 hours.

4. Heat the ghee that was used for frying the onions and add the meat. Fry them for some time on medium heat till the garlic smell is gone. Add the fried onion–garam masala paste and sauté.

5. Boil the milk and add to the meat. Also add 1 cup of water (if required) and cover the vessel and cook on low heat till the meat is tender. Use 1/2 cup of water in case a pressure cooker is used, but they are best slow-cooked.

6. Let the excess water evaporate. The ghee should be visible on top. The texture should be that of a thick paste of masalas on the meat with oil on top. It should not be curry-like.

Shami Kabab

The boiled mincemeat variety of kababs. They taste best with
parathas or roghani tikiya.

Ingredients

1 kg mincemeat or lean meat
150gm or 3/4 cup chana dal
1 cup ghee or oil
1 large onion, chopped
1 inch piece of ginger
4 garlic cloves
5–6 dried red/yellow chillies (or as per taste)*
2 lemons
6 cloves
3 black cardamoms
6–7 peppercorns
1 tsp cumin seeds
1 egg (optional)
Salt to taste

For the stuffing

2 onions, diced into tiny square pieces
5–6 green chillies, finely chopped
1 bunch of coriander leaves, finely chopped

Method

1. Soak the chana dal, preferably overnight or for a few hours.
2. In a pressure cooker, add the mincemeat with all the ingredients except oil and lemons. Add 1/2 cup of water and pressure cook till the meat is done. It is preferable to cook without water. Some cooks use meat pieces instead of mincemeat which takes longer to cook and grind. You can grind your own mincemeat in a mixer-grinder.
3. Let the excess water evaporate and leave it to cool.
4. Dry grind the mincemeat mixture on a sil-batta or in a mixer-grinder. Add lemon juice. A raw egg can be added too to make it crisp.
5. Make patties by putting the stuffing in the middle.
6. Put the patties into the refrigerator for about half an hour to set.
7. Shallow fry the patties in a frying pan and serve them hot.

* In Rampur, yellow chillies are used in place of the red ones.

Chapli Kabab or Kachhey Gosht ki Tikiya

Generally, chapli kabab has a rough, rustic texture, but in Rampur, it has evolved into a smoother kabab; tenderizer is not needed if the meat is absolutely lean and fresh. However, try making one kabab first to check. If it turns out too tough, add tenderizer.

Ingredients

1 kg fine mincemeat
1 cup ghee or oil
1/2 tbsp green papaya paste or 1 tsp tenderizer powder
50 gm parched gram, shelled and powdered
1 large onion, finely diced
1 tbsp ginger paste
1 tbsp garlic paste
1-2 tsp red or yellow chilli powder
10 green cardamoms
3 black cardamoms
1 tsp peppercorns
1 tsp cumin seeds
1 egg
Salt to taste

For the stuffing

2 onions diced into tiny square pieces
5-6 green chillies, finely chopped
1 bunch of coriander leaves, finely chopped

Method

1. Fry the onions in ghee till they turn golden. Drain and remove them. Grind them with the garam masalas (cumin, peppercorn and cardamom) and reserve it.
2. Take the mincemeat in a large bowl and add ginger-garlic pastes, chilli powder (in Rampur, yellow chillies are used),

parched gram powder, papaya paste and salt. Knead them well. Grind the mincemeat if it appears too rough.

3. Add the fried onions and garam masala paste. Mix them thoroughly. Add the egg.

4. Add the stuffing and mix well. Shape into palm-sized, flat, thin patties. They might be irregular.

5. Heat some oil in a frying pan or thick, flat-bottomed pan and fry one patty on simmer to check the softness. If it is too tough, add 1/2 teaspoon of tenderizer and mix it well. In case the patty breaks and is impossible to fry, add breadcrumbs to the mixture.

Five

Gulathhi and First Love

The disappearance of a bowl of gulathhi from the ancient, wheezy refrigerator and Mehrun's elopement were two mysteriously entwined concomitants. Did the creamy rich gulathhi lure the lovers to run away with the sweet bowl? I imagined them sitting in a verdant garden where all runaways go, laughing, their hands dipping into the bowl of creamy delight. The angry outrage at the elopement was fuelled by the loss of the precious sweetmeat sent by our neighbour, a leftover from their daughter's wedding feast. The children had been warned away from the large, earthen bowl of gold–white gulathhi replete with green pistachios, dark raisins and shimmery silver warq. Our family had planned a whole dinner around it—a treat postponed, and ultimately denied.

It all began when one of my kind-hearted aunts decided to take Mehrun along with us to watch the Rekha starrer *Umrao Jaan*. Perhaps, she had earned the treat by making the perfect cup of tea, boiling it thrice over, or had just caught Nikhat khala in an indulgent mood and tagged along. Mehrun, all of fourteen, was enthralled. She wanted to become Umrao Jaan; she obsessively listened to the songs from the film, entertained us with her clumsy imitation of the diva's dance moves, her glass nose pin glinting on her dusky face. Her favourite line was '*Mushkil nahi hai kuchh bhi agar thaan lijiye*' (Nothing is difficult if you are determined). My god-fearing khala was appalled and tried to make Mehrun understand that Umrao Jaan was a 'bad' woman, and such women burn in hell. But, for Mehrun, how could glamour, as against her slovenly life, be bad in any way? Around that time, things started disappearing from the fridge. The vanishing apples and tomatoes were ignored in a family of seven ever-hungry children foraging for snacks in the long, hot summer afternoons. But the disappearance of the gulathhi bowl, stuffed with great effort into the crammed, cavernous fridge, was cataclysmic. It all added up—the stolen moments with her lover and purloined gulathhi, sweet and dreamy as first love.

People generally confuse gulathhi with fereni or even kheer. After all, it is basically a rice-and-milk sweet dish, and how far can one go with the ancient marriage of the simple ingredients. Risking gastronomic snobbishness, I would say that the Rampuri gulathhi differentiates itself as an ostentatious fereni with a peerless twist. The traditional cooks attribute the name 'gulathhi' to the 'gul' or florets, fashioned out of the caramelized scrapings left at the base of the pan, used for garnishing the dish. As for its origin, I'd like to imagine a careless cook in Nawab Rampur's kitchen who didn't stir the fereni pot while it was cooking, and the custard burnt at the bottom of the degh. Maybe he tried damage

control later by using the scrapings as garnish and passing the
smoky flavour off as an innovation. Today, famous gulathhi
cooks, like Munna Bhai, create the 'khurchan' (scrapings) in a
separate pan. They add some gulathhi custard to heated ghee
and let it sizzle to a reddish-brown khurchan for garnish.

Besides the gul trimmings, the method of preparing
gulathhi is very different from the fereni or kheer. The rice
is first boiled in water till tender and mashed before adding
to the milk. Some recipes add a little salt or alum powder to
the boiling rice to ensure that it becomes a grainy paste. For
celebratory occasions, almond and cashew powder are used to
give a rich, nutty flavour and round off the dominant rice taste.
Khoya and cream are also added to the thickening custard.
When the gulathhi has acquired the right consistency, sugar
is sprinkled as per taste. The old texts advocate preparation of
qiwam (sugar syrup) from unrefined sugar and honey. Here is
where fereni ends and gulathhi continues with its surprising,
delicious twist.

A tempering of a sizeable amount of ghee and cardamom
is prepared in a separate pan, and the custard is poured into
it, simmered over low flame, stirred constantly till it acquires
a pinkish-golden blush and begins to congeal at the bottom
of the pan. The scrapings should not be overdone or the
gulathhi will end up with a charred, burnt flavour. The use
of tempering is unique to gulathhi and is never used in its
precursor Persian dish, sheer biranj or fereni.

Gulathhi is finally set in earthenware bowls and garnished
with fried and finely diced cashews, almonds, pistachios,
raisins and the inimitable gul from the khurchan. The freshly
made, large, flat-bottomed clay bowls must be soaked in

water for a few hours so that they don't pull out the moisture from the gulathhi. While the fereni dribbles thickly from the spoon when served, gulathhi forms thick globules. The final consistency is completely different as is the colour. One can only elaborate the intended texture of the dish by the word 'lathh', which would roughly translate to a thick paste that can be smeared—lath-path.

Since it is crucial that the sweetmeat should set well in the bowl, the inexperienced cook tries to achieve the consistency by adding too much rice. This is a cardinal mistake and leads to the regrettable dominance of rice flavour. In fact, dry fruits, kewra water and cardamoms are used to balance the rice aftertaste. The khurchan scrapings give it that unique smoky aroma, which blends into the light, earthy scent of the bowl. The dish has a rich, creamy sophistication which the fereni doesn't aspire to.

The Indian kheer, a sweet dish fit for the gods, has been cooked in the subcontinent for centuries. It is advocated in Ayurveda as a preferred food for good health. The ancient kheer was probably beige in colour as it was made from unpolished rice and sweetened with some form of gur (jaggery) or perhaps honey.[1] Today, the traditional Indian kheer has a grainy texture, and the whole rice grains are cooked in

---

[1] K.T. Acharya in *Historical Dictionary of Indian Food* and in *Indian Food: A Historical Companion* testifies to the presence of jaggery in ancient India; it was mentioned by Kautilya in 300 BC. This challenges the belief that the Portuguese brought sugarcane and jaggery to India.

milk. The fereni tends towards the more homogenous and thick, though still grainy, side due to the use of soaked and ground rice. Renowned food historian K.T. Acharya in his book A *Historical Dictionary of Indian Food* says that the rice used for kheer is lightly fried before boiling with sweetened milk. Kheer made with jowar is mentioned in the fourteenth-century work, *Padmavat*. Shola e zard is another offshoot of the fereni and is a sweet, yellow, rice pudding. It is prepared in Afghanistan and Iran for 'nazr' offering on the tenth day of the holy month of Muharram. Both gulathhi and fereni have their probable antecedents in the Persian sheer biranj that consists of the twin elements of sheer (milk) and biranj (rice). The creation of sheer biranj is said to have revolutionized the basic rice-and-milk pudding by adding rosewater, cardamom and dry fruits and turning it into a cold sweet. However, the Persian sheer biranj doesn't contain sugar and is served with honey or sweet preserves. The Afghani version of sheer biranj has sugar and is similar to gulathhi. Both Persian and Afghani sheer biranj and gulathhi are prepared by first boiling rice in water, which gives credence to their gastronomic liaison with Rampur gulathhi.

Gulathhi finds no mention in the ancient cookbooks on Indo-Persian cuisine dated to the late nineteenth century, preserved at Rampur Raza Library, though there are recipes of the simpler fereni. An interesting recipe of sheerin pulao gulathhi is found in a recipe book, *Haft Khwan Shaukat*, penned by Muhammad Hasan Khan, dated 1883, published in Rampur. The cooking procedure is similar to that of Rampuri gulathhi; the fact that it is classified as a pulao dish indicates the use of ghee and spices. Muhammad Hasan Khan was a food connoisseur from the aristocratic family of Bhopal and was closely connected to Rampur. Thus, gulathhi was a known preparation among the elite families by the end of nineteenth century.

Since gulathhi requires an elaborate list of ingredients, it is more of a celebratory dish cooked at weddings and lavish feasts. After the wedding is over and the bride has left, bowls of gulathhi are zealously guarded. As the sweet dish is highly perishable, the leftovers are presented to close relatives as party favours. Interestingly, gulathhi is rarely cooked for wedding receptions in Rampur because reception dinners are traditionally one- or two-dish meals to feed a large crowd. Rather, it is served by the bride's family at the more elaborate wedding banquet or the chauthi feast, which has a shorter guest list.

The list of ingredients for the gulathhi prepared by Rampuri cooks for my wedding was a long one. I distinctly remember my mother, a non-cooking Rampuri gastronome, read out the list in utter shock—milk, cream, khoya, almond powder, etc. I may be accused of being heavily biased and floating in my own happy haze, but I have never eaten a richer and more perfect gulathhi. I ate several bowls of delectable happiness before my rukhsati. I'm forever grateful to my mother for postponing the going-away ceremony to the morning after the wedding, which gave me the emotional space to gorge on my own wedding feast.

At any banquet, I always take a peek at the sweet dish before settling down to the main course. If it's gulathhi, I eat less of the pulaos and curries. But most of the time, I'm in for a great disappointment; for in Rampur, which is supposedly the last stronghold of gulathhi in its original form, the khansamas have started to cook it like over-gelled fereni. Even the most experienced cooks commit the cardinal error of adding too much rice to help it set. They do try to make it lush by adding khoya, but that cannot salvage the damage done. So these days, I taste a teaspoon of gulathhi first before deciding on skimping on the main course for it.

Speaking to the khansamas who cook gulathhi for the weddings and comparing the recipe with the old family recipe, I discovered horrifying indignities that the original gulathhi is subjected to now. For one, some cooks (I'm trying not to scream out my anger) add the paste of chickpea lentils to the gulathhi along with the rice! They claim that it gives an earthy aroma to the gulathhi and thickens it quickly. Some use tins of condensed milk to skip the long cooking procedure of reducing the milk. Moreover, the cooks no longer bother to create the gul the way it used be done. Today Rampuri gulathhi has become a glorified fereni.

The disappearance of Mehrun (and the gulathhi) broke up the tight, well-greased domestic machinery of our rambling Aligarh home. She had eloped with the cook, Zareena Bua's no-good son, Wamikh. Angry, hysterical scenes and pitched battles in the servants' quarters played out over the next few days; stories were whispered, and half-hearted attempts were made to find Mehrun, for a runaway girl was worthless, spoilt forever. Sabira Bua, Mehrun's prolific, perpetually pregnant mother, cut her losses and married off her younger daughter to Mehrun's fiancé. Zareena Bua, heartbroken and isolated, soon left for Pakistan.

Mehrun, who dominated our days with her cheerful songs, laughter and teasings, disappeared from our immediate consciousness as we got busy—growing up, choosing careers, falling in love—with life. Some said Wamikh left Mehrun and she had a son by him. Since Sabira Bua had moved away with her brood after one of the sons got employed in a government job, we never got any news of Mehrun nor did we hear of the sorely missed curry queen, Zareena Bua. Then, one day in the middle of an aunt's broken elbow emergency, we met Mehrun at the local hospital. With a screech of 'baji', she enveloped my surprised mother and me into a burqa embrace. It took me a minute to recognize the middle-aged woman, her face half obscured by the scarf. The dark eyes dancing with merriment could only be Mehrun's. She had come with her husband, a grave, skinny man with a white scraggly beard. Mehrun had remarried and, as prolific as her mother, had six children of various ages. We exchanged news of marriage, children and a lifetime while they put the plaster on aunt's elbow. More medical emergencies and tragedies awaited us in the womb of the frenzied day, and we lost Mehrun again.

Rampuri Gulathhi Gulzar

The old khansamas always call gulathhi by this elaborate name. After several attempts, I was able to (almost) get the remembered taste of gulathhi with this recipe.

Ingredients

2 litres milk
1 cup sugar (or as per taste)

100 gm basmati rice
75 gm ghee
1 1/4 cup khoya
2 black cardamoms
4 green cardamoms
1/2 tsp kewra water
50 gm almonds, soaked and diced
20 gm pistachios, soaked and diced

Method

1. Wash and soak rice for one hour. Boil the rice in about 1 litre of water till it is absolutely soft. Mash the rice adding a little milk if required. It should be a thick paste. Mix the khoya in 2 cups of milk.
2. Boil the milk and add the rice in small quantities. Keep stirring and boiling the custard till it thickens. Add the khoya milk mixture and keep boiling. It will develop a pinkish hue.
3. Add sugar and kewra water. Keep boiling till the sugar is completely dissolved. Check the gulathhi for its sweetness. Add more sugar if need be.
4. Remove the pan from the fire.
5. Prepare the tempering by heating ghee and adding cardamoms till they crackle. Pour the tempering into the gulathhi and mix well.[2]

---

[2] According to the old recipe, half of the ghee should be heated in another pan and the custard should be poured into it. Then, the tempering should be prepared and added from the top.

6. When the custard cools a little, pour it into deep serving dishes or clay bowls to set. Be sure to soak the clay bowls in water for several hours before using them for the gulathhi.

Preparing the gul

1. The saucepan in which the gulathhi was prepared will have the residue custard. Put the unwashed pan on a skillet over low fire. Close the lid and let it simmer.
2. Check after about 5 minutes. The scrapings will become pinkish. Scrape off an edge from the bottom of the pan. It should be golden. Be careful to not burn the scrapings.
3. Now use a flat spoon to scrape off large chunks of the scrapings. These bits are put on the gulathhi as garnish. Fashion them into little round florets.
4. Garnish it with finely diced almonds and pistachios. Refrigerate before serving.

Six

Piety and Indulgence of Ramzan

'Hazraat! It's time for sehri. Start cooking the khichdi!'

Loudspeakers blare out early morning wake-up calls for sehri interspersed with songs throughout the holy month of Ramzan in the Muslim-dominated old city area of Rampur. Two hours before sehri time, the ladies in the large and small houses that often share a common wall and open into the brick-laid gullies, obediently shuffle towards the kitchens to start off the khichdi. Soon the boys from the neighbouring madrasa begin to clang the door knockers of the houses to ensure that all Muslims are up and about. It's not out of place for a neighbour to drop in to borrow lentils or some other ingredient. The mosques start playing old religious songs followed by announcements counting out the hours and minutes left to the end of sehri time. The noisy clamour throughout the month is tough on the non-fasting populace.

In Rampur, sehri is a complete meal with freshly cooked urad khichdi accompanied by condiments and leftover curries.

The rotis from last night's dinner acquire a yeasty sweet taste and the spices settle into the curries. Everything tastes surreal at that hour. Another favourite is sweet sewain soaked in full-cream milk. My frugal cereal and toast sehri shocks everyone operating on the philosophy of tanking up for the long hours of fast ahead.

I remember the excitement of being woken up for sehri when I was young. It was after a lot of cajoling that Mamma agreed to let me keep roza. Suddenly, I became a part of the secret society of sehri-eaters—dining at an unearthly hour, whisper-talking, stifling giggles and trying not to wake the others up with the kitchen clatter. Mamma, a believer in the power of eggs, would bully me into eating omelettes, which I detested. The day felt so different. I had the lofty status of a rozeydaar—I was spared the little housework I helped out with, and the irritating, young cousins were reprimanded for troubling me. But before I could float into the hallowed circle, Nani Amma would try her best to make me break the fast. She would tempt me with ice-cold sherbet in her special silver katora (bowl), saying that I was too weak for the gruelling fast in the hot weather, and assuring me that Allah would understand. I dodged her attempts, though I knew that a drink from the katora was a very special favour, and rushed off to school, often forgetting all about the roza by lunch time and digging into tiffins and treats. I sometimes see my students saying *tauba, tauba* and patting their cheeks alternately in quick succession when fasting, much like the way I used to repent for inadvertently breaking the fast, uttering a falsehood, or harbouring bad thoughts—we had to be pious all day long or the fast would get 'spoilt'. We tread a thin line with our fragile roza.

Ramzan is also a time of all-night prayers, especially
during the last few nights of Ramzan. Praying together with
the extended family is a tradition I miss—the chai breaks in
the middle of prayers with 'do you remember when . . .' family
stories, the occasional cautionary tales bordering on gossip.
One night, we had a freaky experience; my sister and I were
standing in prayer at home and saw—from the corner of
our eyes—a person behind us, dressed in white, pass by. We
thought it must be one of the aunts, but no one was up yet.
We were told that it was one of the house djinns joining us
for prayers!

The old Ramzan tradition of itikaaf, spending a few nights
in secluded prayers at the mosque, is a ritual followed by
some males in Rampur. Some older women sit in seclusion
at home while the younger ones carry on with their normal
lives, taking care of the house and children alongside fasting.
Sending iftar meals to the mosques and orphanages is a typical
Muslim, and particularly Afghan, tradition followed all over
the world. The mosques and orphanages are flush with funds
since most people want to offer the required amount of zakat
(alms) during Ramzan in the hope of receiving divine blessings
throughout the year.

There is a clear gender split of responsibilities for the
month of fasting. The women, besides their usual duties of
cooking, spend several hours in the bazaars buying clothes for
the entire family. In Rampur, people desire to buy five new
outfits—one for each Friday and a more elaborate one for
Eid. The idea of new clothes for each Friday is rooted in the
concept that everyone is accountable for all their consumption
of food, water and clothes during their lifetime on Judgment

Day. Extending this idea, a majority of Rampuris believe that the clothes made during Ramzan will not be accounted for, so they try to get maximum clothes made during this month! When my father-in-law was alive, all the men in the family received ten new sets of kurta–pyjamas each to last the whole year. In any case, a new dress for Eid is non-negotiable. The bazaars, responding to the new rhythm, open around noon and conduct business till around midnight throughout the month. Sometimes, shopping gets so hectic that women break their fasts in the middle of hectic bargaining. The shopkeepers are well prepared for such eventuality and serve dates and cold drinks to the customers. The men have an even more arduous task at hand—managing the meat supply. The butcher shops transform into an area of frayed tempers and belligerent starving customers—everyone wants the choicest pieces for dinner. Tempers flare with nicotine deprivation. The butchers have their motorcycles close at hand and make a run for it if things get too chaotic.

As a young person, the highlight of my fast was the importance I enjoyed at iftar. In a household of fourteen, we had an eight-seater dining table, with extra chairs added to the sides when required. Food was generally served in two shifts—except iftar. On the day I kept roza, I would be seated on one of the main chairs with everyone fussing over me. The younger siblings and cousins would wait around with their plates, trying to grab some hot pakodis and edge in a side seat. 'Oh, I didn't feel the roza at all. Only felt a bit thirsty', I would beam, hoping for another chance at the privilege of keeping roza.

Around late afternoon or early evening, the ladies and the cooks start off the iftar and dinner preparations. The iftar settles into a daily menu of fritters, fruit kachalu (fruit chaat), boiled black gram or chickpeas with some variations. The rich snacks at iftar leave very little appetite for dinner. A hush descends as the iftar siren sounds and the faithful mimic Prophet Muhammad to break their fast with dates. Though the Prophet could barely afford to eat anything more than dates, and probably milk on a good day, we gulp down lemonade and crunch on hot pakodis, black gram chaat, dahi badas and the syrupy sweet kachalu fruit chaat. The Rooh Afza drink, which used to be equally mandatory on the iftar table as the dates, has become too expensive for regular appearance. However, to cool the overheated stomach, people traditionally soak tukhm e rayan or balanga (basil seeds) to drink as sherbet. Long before the basil-seed fad existed, we were made to gulp down the slimy cool seeds to beat the heat, especially during Ramzan.

Huqqa noshi, the ritual of smoking the communal huqqa (the hubble-bubble pipe) post breaking of the fast, was an ancient cultural practice in Rampur. Described vividly by Asghar Shadani in *Ahwal e Riyasat e Rampur*,[1] the sharing of huqqa was observed in every gher, the central courtyard of the mohalla. The brick-paved common courtyard of the gher was prepared for the post iftar session. To beat the summer heat, it was cooled by spraying water; the huqqa was washed to freshen it—*huqqa taaza karna* as it was called—and a garland of white mogra flowers was entwined around its stem. During the Ramzan month, a special tobacco dipped in molasses was prepared by the tobacconist. A measure of the tobacco was warmed up with coals and put into the huqqa right after iftar. Stools were arranged around the huqqa in a circle and a servant

---

[1] Sayed Asghar Ali Shadani, *Ahwal e Riyasat e Rampur*. Pakistan: Khwaja Printers and Publishers, 2006.

squatted at the centre with the huqqa while another person stood behind the stools. A new, earthen pot filled with cool water and drinking bowls were placed nearby. The smokers, after breaking their fast, took up their positions on the stools or large takhts. The servant passed the huqqa to the first person, probably based on his seniority or position in the mohalla. The person would take one or two small puffs, warming up, and then take three long puffs. The effect of the tobacco right after the fast would hit the patriarch, and he would fall backwards only to be caught as he fell and revived by the cool water. Once the dizzy spell passed, he would get up, stretch and go for his dinner. Then the huqqa was passed to the second person in the pecking order and so on. My mother told me that my grandfather also smoked the huqqa in the gher in this manner. The huqqa noshi gatherings continued in most mohallas till the eighties withstanding the charm of the quick-fix cigarettes. Then it slowly phased out. My guess is that the pull of the post-liberalization television proved stronger than the delights of all-male evening baithaks. But there are still pockets in the bazaar where there is evening catch-up and sharing over cups of tea.

Ramzan is marked by a series of delectable iftar dinners, often with relatives and friends. From cosy home dinners to grand feasts held in banquet halls, it's a busy social calendar. But all that starts in the second half of the month. During the first half, the men are engaged in listening to the Quranic recitations in the hour-long nightly tarawih prayers before they sit down to a well-deserved late dinner. Few women go for the tarawih prayers though there are special women's-only section in the Jama Masjid. Several Rampur families train at least one of their sons to become a hafiz (who memorizes and recites the Quran) in the hope that the hafiz son will lead the

parents into heaven. The schools, too, give a month's leave
to the hafiz students because they have to recite the Quranic
verses at the tarawih prayers. The custom is so rooted in
Rampur and the adjoining areas that the children chosen as
hafiz do not attend normal school till they have completed
the memorization of the verses. These students are around
nine to eleven years of age and the schools admit them to the
classes according to their age; they cope quite well with their
studies. I have observed that they carry themselves differently,
conscious of the piety thrust upon them and the burden of
carrying their beloved parents to the Kingdom of Heaven.

Faith and feasts converge to deliver the most perfect
iftar meals throughout the month of Ramzan to appease the
humble minds that fill with food cravings and gastronomical
thoughts through the day. Right from iftari to the late
dinner meal, the palate celebrates the return to pleasure of
a well-thought-out, perfectly synchronized meal. Rampur's
cuisine is traditionally served in combinations which might
not seem logical—kadhi and rice is somewhat strangely
combined with meatballs in spicy gravy; pulao dictates a
kabab and dahi bada combination; mincemeat with besan
(gram chickpea flour) roti is another favourite; and whole
urad is cooked with meat combined with fried, aromatic
rice. The conventional food groupings—learned through
food narratives—with their complimentary tastes, ensure
satiation of a rewarding meal after a day spent in piety. In
the early years of my marriage, I used to spend some part of
the month at my in-laws' place in the old city. The flavour
of Ramzan—from a noisy sehri to sumptuous iftar—is quite
distinctive there.

As the time for iftari draws near, everyone is seized with cravings and the men are cajoled to get chaat, kababs and the inimitable qeema samosa—the iconic crisp triangle filled with spicy mincemeat urgently fried at only a few shops right before sunset, a special iftar snack. The supply is limited and the menfolk, pious and ravenous, queue up at 'Famous', 'Mashooq Bhai' or 'Amanat Bhai's' outlets. The samosas come piping hot to the iftar table in newspaper packets to gladden the hearts of starving family members. The older generation remarks that the qeema samosas tasted far better earlier and the shops don't use the proper meat any longer. For me the greasy, crisp samosa with the spices and green chilli laden meaty centre is beyond perfection.

It is said that the samosa originated from the Central Asian traveller's snack, samsa. The Uzbek samsa, the Persian sanbosag, or the Arabic sambusak are very similar to our samosa; they are either baked or fried, the pastry often thicker and sprinkled with sesame seeds. Filled with mincemeat and roasted over campfire, the samosa was brought to India by traders and it became a favoured item in the fourteenth century. Muhammad Bin Tughlaq ate a mincemeat and dry fruit filled samosa with the pulao. The love affair with the mincemeat samosa continued during the Mughal period described in *Ain i Akbari*. When the Portuguese introduced potatoes in India, the tuber found its way into the sanbusa—as it was called in *Ain i Akbari*—which might have made it popular among the vegetarian populace. Possibly, samosas started being fried rather than baked in India. Its ancestors are still baked in Central Asia.

The following poem was recorded by Mas'udi, one of the first Arab historians, in his historical work *Meadows*

of Gold, written in 947 CE, on sanbusak, translated into
English by Arthur John Arberry in his book *Aspects of Islamic
Civilization*.

> . . . *And when the burning flames have dried it quite,*
>> *Then, as thou wilt, in pastry wrap it round,*
>> *And fasten well the edges, firm and sound;*
>> *Or, if it please thee better, take some dough,*
>> *Conveniently soft, and rubbed just so,*
>> *Then with a rolling-pin let it be spread*
>> *And with the nails its edges docketed.*
>> *Pour in the frying pan the choicest oil*
>> *And in that liquor let it finely broil . . .*

Interestingly, the snack so enamoured the Rampur Nawabs
that a dish called samosa pulao was prepared for the Nawab's
table. The dish was probably learnt from or cooked by chefs
from Delhi as similar recipes are found in old Delhi cookbooks
dating late-nineteenth century. The samosa pulao was the
yakhni pulao garnished with crisp qeema-filled samosas.
We can only imagine the crunchy samosas complimenting
the sublime yakhni pulao. Samosa pulao, along with other
varieties of the inimitable yakhni pulao, exists only in food
archives now.

In the manuscript recipes, the qeema samosas were first
steamed like momos and then fried. The pastry of the samosa
was prepared by kneading refined flour, chickpea flour and
egg white. For the filling, the mincemeat, mixed with spices,
was half-cooked, ground and filled into the triangles made
from the pastry batter. The samosas were then wrapped in

betel leaves and steamed over a degh to harden the crust. Finally, the betel leaves were cut away and the samosas were shallow-fried. The recipe is more complex than our simple everyday samosa.

Last year, my nephew tried vainly to get qeema samosa during Ramzan, but Amanat Bhai disappointed us due to, he said, 'unavailability of proper meat'. I attempted to make the samosas from leftover mincemeat, even tried the ready-to-fry qeema samosas, but they lacked the zest and bite of Amanat Bhai's creations.

Ramzan had a different texture in 2020, the year of the COVID-19 pandemic and lockdowns. The bazaars and mosques were bare of the usual finery of filigree and fairy lights. Since there were no nightly tarawih prayers, the men wanted food almost immediately after iftar, which meant no breather for the women. Though there was home delivery of chicken meat, the butcher shops remained closed, robbing the males of their arena of pugnacious venting. The bazaars were shut down too, and the women fretted over Eid dresses. There was a rumour that the popular tailors, 'Merino Bhai' and 'A to Z Bhai', referred to by the names of their establishments, had set up their workshops secretly at their residences. Smart women, who had shopped for cloth earlier, managed to send their dresses there. Shopping for clothes online was resorted to by the youngsters. The older generation, who preferred to buy after feeling the material and trying on the dresses, felt uncomfortable buying online. There was barely any street food to satisfy cravings, so the women were coaxed into cooking chaat and samosas, while the younger members helped out with YouTube instructions.

We suffered another samosa-less Ramzan. As Amir Khusrau's famous riddle goes:

Samosa kyon na khaaya? Joota kyon na pehna?
Jawaab: Talaa na tha!

(Why wasn't the samosa eaten? Why wasn't the shoe worn?
Answer: The samosa wasn't fried [talaa]; the shoe didn't have a sole [also talaa].)

Some Iftar Snacks

Qeema Samosa

Even with the best of my efforts, I can never replicate Amanat Bhai's samosas. Mutton mincemeat is the best stuffing for this because chicken meat tastes too bland in the samosa.

Ingredients

For about 20 medium-sized samosas

For the filling

300 gm lean mincemeat

2 tbsp refined oil
1 onion, finely diced
2 tsp ginger–garlic paste
2 tsp red chilli powder
1/2 tsp turmeric powder
1/2 tsp coriander powder
4 chillies, finely chopped
Salt to taste

For the samosas

2 cups refined flour
1 tsp salt
1 cup water
Oil for deep frying[2]

Method

1. First, prepare the samosa batter by mixing salt with refined flour. Knead the flour, adding water gradually. Cover the dough and set it aside for 10 minutes.
2. Divide the dough into equal portions and make thin rotis by flattening the dough with a rolling pin. Cut each roti into four wedges and set aside.
3. Make a 'glue' paste by mixing about 2 teaspoon refined flour with 1/2 a bowl of water. It should have a smooth consistency.

---

[2] The quantity depends on the depth of your kadhai.

4. Prepare the filling: heat the oil, add ginger–garlic paste and sauté for some time.
5. Add the mincemeat and sauté.
6. Put in the red chilli, coriander and turmeric powders and salt. Keep sautéing till the qeema becomes a little tender. If it is still hard, consider adding 1/2 cup of water and cook till the water evaporates and the mincemeat becomes tender. However, adding water is not recommended.
7. Add the chillies and the diced onions and sauté till onions become slightly soft. Set aside.

Preparation

1. Take a samosa pastry wedge and make a cone, sealing the overlapping edges with the glue paste. Put the filling into the pocket and seal the mouth. Set it aside.
2. After preparing all the samosas, deep fry them in piping hot oil till they turn golden. Drain the samosas and put them on tissues to remove the excess oil. Serve with red chilli and garlic chutney.

Dahi Phulki

Dahi Phulki reminds me of a Rampuri aphorism of getting along well—*jaisey dahi mein phulki*. Here's to getting along swimmingly!

Ingredients

For the phulkis

100 gm gram flour
1 medium-sized onion, finely chopped
1 tbsp onion paste
1 tsp red or yellow chilli powder
3–4 green chillies, finely chopped
1/2 to 1 cup water
2 cups refined oil
1/2 tsp baking soda
Salt to taste

For the curd

1tsp cumin powder
1/4 tsp garlic
4–5 red or yellow chillies
1 tsp salt

For the garnish

1/2 a bowl of chopped coriander
1 tsp cumin powder

Method

1. Prepare the gram chickpea flour or besan batter by adding baking powder, salt, chillies and onion paste to it. Add

water and whisk till it is of a thick but runny consistency. It is important to whisk it really well. A drop of the batter should float when added to a bowl of water.

2. Add the chopped onions and green chillies and set aside for an hour.

3. For the curd: grind the spices in a blender with a little water.

4. Strain the curd through the flour sieve to ensure a homogenous texture. Add the spices into the curd and mix it well. Check the salt. Set it aside.

5. Heat the oil in a deep kadhai on high flame. When it is heated well, lower the flame to medium and drop 1/2 tablespoon of batter for one pakodi. Make in batches of as many pakodis as the pan can accommodate.

6. When the fritters are golden brown, remove from the oil using a perforated ladle and drop them into a bowl of water and allow the pakodis to soak in the water for about 10 minutes.

7. When the fritters are all done, softly squeeze the water out and put into the prepared curd.

8. Garnish the dish with coriander and sprinkle some cumin powder on top.

Kala Chana Chaat

This is a very common preparation all over India. It is a popular, high-protein iftar snack.

Ingredients

1/2 cup kala chana (black chickpeas)
1/2 tbsp cooking oil
1/2 tsp cumin seeds
1/4 tsp asafoetida (optional)
1 medium-sized onion, finely chopped
1/2 tsp chaat masala powder
1 lemon
Salt to taste
Water as required

Method

1. Wash and soak the black chickpeas in water overnight or for around 8–10 hours.
2. Drain the water and cook the chickpeas in a pressure cooker by adding salt and 2 cups of water.
3. Pressure cook them for 3–4 whistles on low flame. If they are still tough, then add water, if required, and cook for 1–2 whistles more.
4. Drain the boiled chickpeas and keep aside.
5. Heat oil in a kadhai or pan. Add asafoetida and cumin seeds. When the seeds begin to splutter, add the chopped onions and cook until they turn translucent.
6. Put in the chopped green chilli. Mix them well and sauté them for about 10 seconds on low flame.
7. Add the black gram and mix everything together. Let it simmer for about 5 minutes.
8. Add chaat masala and lemon juice. Garnish the dish with chopped onions. Serve it hot.

Seven

Eid Sweets and Disasters

Hai Eid maekadey ko chalo dekhta hai kaun,
Shahad o shakar pe toot padey rozeydaar aaj.

(It's Eid, let us sneak into the tavern unobserved,
The faithful are busy feasting on sugar and honey.)
—Nawab Sayed Yusuf Ali Khan Nazim
of Rampur (ruled 1855–1865)

Attu Bhai's qiwami sewain used to be the first culinary disaster on tense Eid mornings. They either came out too sweet, curling into shocked turgidity, angry red from the colour he added to hide their uncompromising stance, or they would be at the other end of the spectrum—too soft, lumpy and barely sweet. Rescue operations were immediately launched—pouring sugar syrup or adding milk to make them softer and palatable. Once, we even put the inedible mass into a pressure cooker!

'Uffo, Attu, your sewain is as tough as your hair!', Nani Amma would despair.

Attu Bhai had black, tightly curled hair, and from then on, the texture of qiwami sewain inhabited a hairy area in my mindscape; I despised the dish and avoided it through my childhood and early youth.

Attu Bhai was one among a large brood of orphans brought up by my great-grandmother. All of them grew up to be a band of loyal servants around 'Kaptanni Bibi' (wife of 'kaptaan' or captain), who delighted in arranging their weddings, celebrating the birth of their children, and admonishing and rewarding them like a benign, despotic queen. After her death, most of her adoptive children were settled into different professions by my grandfather. Attu Bhai remained with us for the longest time, graduating from an odd-job boy to finally managing the kitchens—skills reluctantly taught by Haji Bakka, our old khansama. The latter, like the quintessential Rampuri cook, didn't reveal all his secrets to Attu, leaving us mourning for his curries and kababs when he retired. There was always an essential ingredient, a fine print of sub-procedure missing from Attu Bhai's cooking. In the Attu era, the kitchen became a dank, barely clean place, and the meals had an unpredictable taste. Finally, a position was found for Attu Bhai in the Aligarh Muslim University kitchens, and the household heaved a sigh of relief.

Demonstrating his love and undying loyalty, Attu Bhai would make his Eid appearance and insist on making qiwami sewain. My Nani Amma was an armchair cook and a vehement dining table food critic, and so the daughters-in-law were too scared to take on the onerous task of preparing large

quantities of the signature Eid dish. We ate or avoided Attu
Bhai's inflexible, over-sweet sewain till Nani Amma passed
away and the daughters-in-law gently took away Attu Bhai's
privilege. When I first ate the 'real' qiwami sewain at a friend's
place in Lucknow, with the sugary qiwam dripping from the
fine, delicately stewed strands, I immediately got over my
gastronomic trauma and submitted to a lifelong affair with
the syrupy, melty vermicelli dish.

Qiwami sewain entails the cooking of sewain in sugar
syrup or qiwam. It is essentially an Awadhi and Mughlai dish
and was probably imported into Rampur as it does not feature
in the list of sweet meats in most of the Rampur culinary
archives. A mid-twentieth-century recipe book on royal dishes
describes the method of preparation that is very different from
our practice in Rampur. The sewain is fried, put into a muslin
cloth and blanched in boiling water, just enough to make it
soft. Then it is combined with sugary qiwam, slow cooked in
a sealed pan and put on dum. We don't blanch the vermicelli
anymore, but some cooks do put a bit of water or milk into
the fried vermicelli to make it soft before the onslaught of
sugar syrup. The qiwami sewain requires a skilful balancing
of sweetness and texture, each glistening strand separate from
the other, never crisp, and with the syrup forming a glistening
halo around the sewain. In the hands of the inexperienced,
the sweet syrup poured over the fried vermicelli might make
the thin strands recoil and curl up in inflexible horror. The
master chefs can cook the dish with up to eight times (athguni)
weight of sugar to that of the vermicelli. We manage double
strength sugar syrup (duguni) sewain with great difficulty.
Our Attu Bhai attempted the classic chauguni sewain—the

Deghs of gosht roti being prepared for the *dawat e walima* (wedding banquet) in the kitchen shed of a *shadi ghar* (wedding venue).

Nawab Sayed Hamid Ali Khan (1894–1930).

Mr Ameer Ahmad Khan, chief secretary to the Nawab and electrical engineer of Riyasat Rampur, examining a fighting cockerel in Rampur bazaar. The picture dates to the 1960s.

Photo credit: Sadaf Hussain

Boti kababs being barbecued over coals.

Photo credit: Tarana Husain Khan

Raan kabab prepared by marinating leg of goat or sheep and then slow cooking over coals.

Photo Credit: Zameer Ahmad

Nargisi koftas have the yellow centre and white penumbra resembling the narcissus flower, hence the name. The skill is to ensure that the mince adheres to the boiled eggs and the kofta doesn't disintegrate in the curry.

Seekh kabab nargisi is a variation of the usual seekh kababs. It has rings of boiled egg whites encircling the seekh kabab. A skillful preparation by traditional Rampuri kababis.

Photo Credit: Zameer Ahmad

A rare picture of a dastarkhwan being laid out on low tables for a dawat in Khasbagh Palace in the 1950s. At the head of the centre table is Nawab Syed Raza Ali Khan with eminent members of Rampur seated near him. The formal meals were usually served on dining tables.

Hamid Manzil, the erstwhile Durbar Hall of Rampur Riyasat. It is now the Raza Library, the repository of manuscripts, books, paintings and artifacts collected by successive Nawabs of Rampur. The picture dates to the beginning of the twentieth century.

Wright Gate, named after Mr W. C. Wright, the chief engineer of Rampur who undertook the construction of several state buildings under Nawab Sayed Hamid Ali Khan. In a garden inside the qila, there used to be a life-sized statue of Mr Wright, which disappeared a few years ago. The picture dates to 1905.

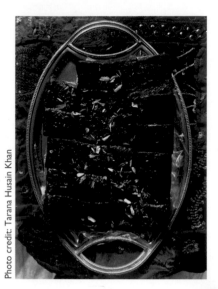

Halwa Sohan is a delectable sweetmeat of Rampur prepared from samnak (wheatgerm flour)

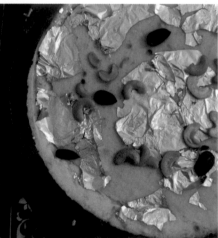

Rampuri gulathhi is a richer version of the ancient rice and milk sweetmeat, which has several variations all over the country.

Safeda is a sweet rice preparation generally served at walima banquets in Rampur.

proportion of sugar to sewain being four to one—and failed every time. Muneeza Shamsie, daughter of Begum Jahanara, in her article 'Muneeza Shamsie: My family's culinary history across India, Pakistan and Britain'[1] describes a very different recipe of qiwami sewain cooked in her home. It involves cooking sewain in qiwam, cream and condensed milk before finally baking it in the oven—a traditional recipe with a sumptuous modern twist. The oversweet qiwami sewain is to be relished in small portions often with fresh cream.

Most Rampuri household have a shortcut, simple style of cooking the dish. They don't prepare the sugar syrup. Instead, the fried sewain is blitzed with sugar, water and milk. It turns out well but never as magnificent as the painstakingly cooked qiwami sewain. The food puritans don't call it qiwami sewain since it does not entail making sugar syrup or qiwam. A similar recipe is described by the Pakistani food writer Bisma Tirmizi. I found the same recipe in Lucknow cuisine cookbooks too. Somewhere along the way, the simple, abbreviated method of cooking the dish became more popular and the strands of vermicelli became thicker to accommodate it.

The sewain probably originated from the Greek and Turkish kataifi pastry made from unleavened dough, sieved through a perforated plate into thin strands and roasted over heated metal plates. Kataifi pastry, a softer version of our sewain, is packed into airtight bags and frozen. It is used as the base for the celebrated baklava, kanafeh as well as savoury dishes in Greek, Turkish and Middle Eastern cuisines.

---

[1] The article was published in the 'Forgotten Foods' series of articles in *Scroll.in* magazine.

Begum Jahanara Habibullah describes the preparation of sewain pastry in Rampur homes before Eid in her memoir. The wheat dough was squeezed through a perforated wooden contraption, and the thin strands separated and hung out to dry on trees. Thus, the texture, the ingredients and the methodology of preparing the kataifi and sewain are similar. Both the pastries are baked or fried and put into sugar syrup, and the thin strands allowed to absorb the sweetness. The Turkish and the Palestinian kanafeh has the look and the texture of our qiwami sewain with the fried and baked kataifi pastry drizzled with sugar syrup. The only distinguishing factor is that the kanafeh has soft goat cheese sandwiched between layers of vermicelli. The kataifi vermicelli is a pliable and highly versatile pastry and can be shaped into baklava rolls filled with dry fruits soaked in sugar syrup or honey, as well as savoury seafood rolls. Indian vermicelli, by contrast, is crisp, brittle and used to make two types of Eid dishes—qiwami sewain and sheer khurma (sewain cooked in milk and dates). The less sweet option of qiwami sewain is muzaffar, prepared with liberal use of saffron. Incidentally, muzaffar denotes the use of saffron and the term is also used for sweet rice cooked with saffron.

Begum Jahanara Habibullah writes that on Eid-ul-Fitr, after the communal Eid prayers at the Jama Masjid, her father used to break his fast with sheer khurma, as did everyone else. Shaista Ikramullah's work, *Behind the Veil: Ceremonies, Customs and Colour*[2], echoes the same practice followed at the

---

[2] Shaista Suhrawardy Ikramullah. *Behind the Veil: Ceremonies, Customs and Colour*. Pakistan: Oxford University Press, 1994.

Mughal and Lucknow courts in the late-nineteenth century. Sheer khurma, a milk-based sewain, was traditionally the Eid breakfast dish and the first sweet to pass the lips of the faithful on Eid day. It was a lifesaver in Attu Bhai years. It's a simple dish consisting of two main ingredients—milk (sheer) and dates (khurma). The milk is boiled, and the dates, dry fruits and sugar are added to the milk base. Sewain is used to add a certain consistency to the dish. Probably sewain was amalgamated to the simple milk-and-dates Middle Eastern sweet as it travelled through the land of the versatile kataifi pastry or, maybe, the two were married in the court of the Turkish Delhi Sultans. One would incline towards the latter as the Indian subcontinent style sheer khurma is not found in Turkish or Middle Eastern cuisines.

My mother is a one-dish cook on Eid, just like loyal Attu. Sheer khurma is still the first dish cooked at home, and Mamma, more comfortable in the operation theatre than the kitchen, takes charge like a surgeon with at least one assistant and the ingredients arranged in a proper order around the stove. Face sweating from the steam from the bubbling milk, she peers into the large deghchi, thrusts out a hand and commands, 'coconut!', 'sewain!', 'sugar!' The ingredients are handed over like scalpels, scissors and clamps, the assistant swabbing her brow intermittently. We break our fast with her peerless sheer khurma on Eid mornings. It is a 'can't go wrong' dish most of the time, but that can't be taken for granted. Once, the milk curdled when I added the raisins because they were slightly sour. I add the raisins right at the end now.

Eid mornings in Rampur, as everywhere else, are always chaotic. The men, all bathed and dressed in sparkling new kurta–pyjamas, leave for morning Eid prayers with their prayer mats tucked under their arms. If they are early, they get a place inside the mosque, or else they have to spread their mats on the roads where the spill over from the mosque line up. The roads are painted with slanting white lines to indicate the direction of the Kaaba and all traffic is directed away from the roads around the mosque.

The men celebrate Eid in different ways than women. I have only heard of their Eid sequence—hugging their friends and acquaintances after the communal prayer, giving alms to the beggars, visiting the graves of ancestors and Sufi saints, revelling in wholly different outside-Eid celebrations before returning to their women involved in different stages of cooking and laying out the Eid delicacies. I barely manage to cook sewain, chickpeas and dahi dumplings before they are back. I think most ladies accept the Eid greetings from their men drenched in sweat. But there are few super-efficient ladies who cook through the night and still manage to sit all dolled up at the laid-out Eid table. The men 'break their fast' with sweet sewain. My Nani Amma used to recite the fatiha prayers over the Eid table—simple Quranic prayers followed by a prayer for the souls of the ancestors—while all her children and grandchildren dressed in their Eid finery stood around the table, hands raised in prayer. It was a quaint ritual, which we abandoned after Nani Amma passed away because our 'rediscovered' Islam, from Gulf literature and lectures, shunned such traditions as blasphemous innovations.

As a young person, my job was to dust the drawing room and arrange flowers while the aunts, cooks and my mother struggled in the kitchen. Winter Eids were easier as I could arrange roses, but summer Eids required consultation of the old Ikebana book to arrange the dry-looking zinnias and the foliage. Years later, my sister, who got married and settled in Dubai, was shocked to see women joining the men in offering Eid namaz at the mosque and attending Eid parties afterwards.

Eid celebrations at the royal court of Rampur were elaborate affairs with mubarakbadi or congratulatory songs sung in raag Durbari. The naubat orchestra with the musicians seated in the gallery above the palace gates was played after the Eid namaz at the Jama Masjid. The mardana (males only) durbar was held at Hamid Manzil durbar hall,[3] where the courtiers presented nazar—a gold coin on a handkerchief proffered on both the palms to the Nawab. The zenana (female) durbar was held at the Sheesh Mahal in the qila (fort). Her Highness Begum Rampur, the chief queen, accepted greetings and nazar from the noblewomen. The offering of nazar was an ancient Muslim court custom to pay tribute to a sovereign. The dress code in both the durbars was formal—shervanis for men and farshi ghararas[4] for women.

Eid festivities and Eid visits carry on for three days after Eid. In Rampur, several schools are forced to declare a three-day holiday because rickshaw and bus drivers go on leave. The visits follow a strict protocol. The 'younger' relatives, a derivative of relationship rather than chronological age, visit their elders and receive Eidi or Eid gift in the form of money. It is extremely important to visit the house of mourning where there has been a death in the past year.

---

[3] The present Raza Library.
[4] Shervani is a long coat worn by men. Gharara is a two-legged skirt worn by women.

Children are the beneficiaries of Eid visits and tag along to increase their bounty. They base their opinions about the prosperity, generosity and love of various relatives on the Eidi given to them. Siblings and cousins exchange notes later—'Papa's relatives are more generous', 'Aunt so-and-so is a miser' etc. The sons-in-law and daughters-in-law get the highest amount. The going rate for Eidi has changed drastically over the years. Nani Amma used to give us crisp two-rupee notes saying they were the prettiest currency— pink with the lion emblem. As a child, my daughter would give away her Eidi collection to her cousins in exchange for Eid salaam. She loved to sit, make her senior cousins line up for Eidi and bow deep in salaam. The children played along to increase their largesse.

2020 was a year of lockdown Eids in the shadow of pandemic tragedies. Though only five people were allowed for Eid namaz, the administration could not restrain the sheer physicality of Eid greetings—the three hugs defied all social distancing. In a town where houses lean on each other—often sharing a wall, clustered around a common gher—it is easy to sneak into the house of extended family members and hold friends and relatives close to the heart in an embrace. No one could manage to visit us in Civil Lines, but we went for our Eid visit to my brother-in-law's place in the old city as soon as we could.

The Eid after Ramzan fasts is called meethi Eid by non-Muslims although both Eids have sewain preparations. The reason for the epithet is to distinguish it from Eid ul-Adha or Bakra Eid which entails animal sacrifice. Our non-Muslim friends rarely drop in on Bakra Eid.

During the time of the Nawab and till the 1960s, there was a separate open area where people could get the sacrifice done. Most men performed the act themselves—it was considered a proof of masculinity. Some just touched the animal with the dagger or said a prayer. Maybe it is the lack of open spaces or stricter rules, people have started performing the qurbani inside their courtyards, leaving the offals in the open drains. The city stinks to high heaven after Eid, and I pity the vegetarian populace living in the inner mohallas.

We used to have the qurbani in our ancestral home in Aligarh where there was a lot of land all around. Often, goats were reared there, and we were asked to feed the goats so that we felt the pain of sacrifice. After the qurbani, the servants would sit with piles of meat and weighing scales and distribute the meat under the supervision of an aunt—the mandatory percentage that should go to the poor, the choicest pieces to the in-laws and close relatives; the carefully orchestrated exchange of meat portions between families. Which family gave how much and what kind of meat was to be given were coded rules and conventions. I could never eat the meat dishes prepared post-Eid. Raan musallam, goat brain curry and liver–kidney curry are the favourite preparations after Eid. Sons-in-law, brothers-in-law and close relatives are called over for dinner on the days following Eid and the refrigerators are overstocked with meat portions, which last for days in the hands of the prudent housewife.

Qiwami Sewain

I learned this old-style qiwami sewain from my friend Samina Naqvi in Allahabad. Very few families cook qiwami sewain in this manner.

Ingredients

250 gm sewain[5]
500 gm sugar (or as per taste)
100 gm khoya, grated
1 cup or 250 gm ghee
1 cup milk
6 whole green cardamoms
25 gm almonds, soaked and chopped
20 gm raisins, soaked
10 gm charoli seeds (chironji)
1/4 tsp saffron
4–5 drops kewra water
Silver leaf for decoration (optional)

Method

1.　Take 1 cup of water in a pan, pour the sugar in it and put it on heat to make qiwam or sugar syrup. Keep stirring it intermittently till it thickens. It shouldn't be too viscous or the sewain will suffer. Take a slightly cooled blob of syrup and test it by pulling it between the thumb and

---

[5]　I prefer to use the very thin Banarasi sewain. Try to get as thin sewain pastry as possible.

index finger. It should be sticky and one taar or strand should be visible.

2. Warm the milk. Soak the saffron in 1 tablespoon of warm milk.

3. Heat the ghee in a large saucepan.[6] Add the green cardamoms. Stir them till they crackle. Lower the heat to a medium flame. Then add the sewain and fry them till they are golden red. (The sewain shouldn't burn or become brown or the final dish would have a dark colour. Take care not to break the sewain.)

4. Arrange the fried sewain in a uniform layer and pour the hot qiwam over it, taking care to soak the entire sewain layer. Immediately add the milk. The mixture will roll to a little boil in a few seconds. Turn off the flame. The dish will be a bit liquidy but the liquid will get absorbed in the sewain. Check if the sewain is soft. If it is not (like Attu Bhai's), add a little hot water and let it simmer for a few seconds.

5. Add the grated khoya and mix it. Sprinkle the saffron milk and kewra water all over it in a circular motion. Then mix it gently.

6. Put it in a serving bowl and garnish the dish with dry fruits and decorate with the silver leaf. Make sure not to leave the sewain in the hot saucepan or it will dry out.

---

[6] The bottom of the pan should be large enough to spread the sewain in a layer.

Sheer Khurma

This is of course my mother's recipe—the only one she ever
taught me.

Ingredients

2 litres full cream milk
100 gm sewain
250 gm sugar (or as per taste)
1 cup milk
2 tbsp ghee
100 gm or 1/2 tin of Milkmaid condensed milk[7]
10–12 green cardamoms
10–12 dates, chopped lengthwise
15 gm almonds, soaked in water and chopped roughly
20 gm raisins, soaked in water
Half a coconut, cut in small square pieces and soaked
10 gm chironji
10 gm cashews, soaked and chopped roughly
1/2 tsp saffron
A pinch of salt

Method

1. Boil the milk for about 20 minutes till it reduces. Add
   cashews, coconut and almonds. Keep boiling it till the dry

---

[7] Puritans shun the use of condensed milk. My family translates it to lack of
effort and claim that the sheer doesn't taste the way it should. If I have the
time, I increase the milk by a litre and double the boiling time. The sugar
also needs to be increased.

fruits are tender. Add cardamom seeds; use the seeds and skin separately.

2. Heat the ghee in a frying pan and sauté sewain lightly till they turn golden.

3. Add sewain to the milk. Add chironji and dates. You may use dried dates (chowara) instead of fresh ones. Soak them overnight.

4. Immediately add condensed milk, sugar and a pinch of salt. Let it simmer for a few minutes and turn off the stove.

5. Add soaked raisins after draining the water. Add saffron.

6. Pour in a serving bowl and keep it in the refrigerator to cool. The consistency should be thick, not watery.

Dahi Bada

Rampuri dahi bada is an aspirational dish. They are flat, thin and palm-sized; soft enough to be 'eaten with the lips', fluffy and well done at the centre. They are never thick and spongy like the dahi badas we eat with chaat. Though mine are never perfectly round or palm-sized, they come close to perfection but are not good enough to garner a culinary reputation.

Ingredients

For the badas

250 gm white urad dal,[8] soaked overnight
1 tsp garlic paste
1 tsp ginger paste
1 tsp garam masala powder
1 tsp red or yellow chilli powder
1/2 tsp soda powder
1 tsp asafoetida
2 tsp salt
500 ml refined oil

For the curd

500 gm curd
3-4 yellow or red chillies
1-2 tsp garlic paste
Cumin seeds
1 tsp salt

Method

1. Wash and soak urad dal overnight. Next morning, drain
   the water and grind the dal without using any water. Use

---

[8] The food puritans use split black urad. They soak it overnight and remove
the black skins the next day by washing the dal vigorously and fishing the
skins that float on top of the water. It does taste better. If you are a true
foodie, try the hard way!

a grinder but it is preferable to use the grindstone (sil-batta). The consistency should be of soft-kneaded dough. It should be absolutely smooth, not grainy.

2. Add garlic–ginger pastes, garam masala, soda and chilli powder. Do not add salt. Mix them well and set the dough aside for about 1 hour to let the soda work in the dough.

3. In a large bowl, take about 1 litre of water and mix salt and asafoetida to dunk the badas in.

4. Heat the oil in a kadhai for deep frying (shallow frying is also an option). Take a little portion of the batter and make flat cakes on the palm of the hand. To avoid stickiness, dip the fingers lightly in water while making the cakes. In case the batter becomes runny, break 2–3 bread slices and knead into the batter. Slip the badas gently into the hot oil. Fry them on low heat till they turn golden brown (not too dark). Take out the badas and dunk them into the salt water for some time to make them soft.

5. After all the badas are fried and put into the water, gently squeeze them between the palms to drain the water and set them on the serving dish. If they are to be served later, put them into a bowl and refrigerate.

6. Prepare the curd by sieving and whipping it. Grind the chillies and garlic into a paste and add to the curd along with salt. Alternately, or if in a hurry, garlic paste and chilli powder can be used.

7. Sauté cumin seeds on skillet till they crackle and grind them to get 2 teaspoon of cumin powder.

8. Pour the curd over the badas till they are completely covered.[9] Garnish the dish with sautéed and ground cumin powder and sprigs of dhania.

Raan Musallam

This is one post Eid dish I feel confident about. I marinate it for at least 24 hours, taking it out of the fridge several times and pricking it all over to make the masalas settle into the meat. Majid khansama helped us fashion a special three-pronged skewer for barbecuing it.

Ingredients

Leg of goat or lamb (raan)
4 onions, diced fine
3 tbsp garlic paste
2 tbsp ginger paste
6 tbsp red vinegar (or juice of 4 lemons) or 3/4 cup curd
6 tbsp ghee
2 tsp garam masala powder
2 tbsp cream
2–3 tbsp raw papaya paste

---

[9] Tip: Add an exotic Nawabi touch by smoking the curd. Put a glowing coal on a piece of roti. Place it on top of the dahi badas. Pour a tablespoon of ghee. Cover it if possible. Remove the coal after it cools down.

2–3 tsp red chilli powder

2 tsp salt (or as per taste)

Method

1. Wash the raan thoroughly. Trim off the fatty layers. Make deep gashes all over it. Rub vinegar on it.

2. Mix ginger, garlic, garam masala, raw papaya, chilli powder and salt. Slather it all over the raan. Rub it and gash the raan with knife once again.[10]

3. Put in a covered bowl or use tin foil to cover. A minimum of 6 hours marination is required. A 24-hour marination in the fridge is highly recommended.

4. Take out after 12 hours and prick it once again. Add cream and yoghurt, rubbing all over. Turn the raan. Put it back in the refrigerator.

5. Fry the diced onions till crisp and golden. Drain and spread on a kitchen towel. Crush the onions and paste all over the raan. Pour ghee on it.

6. Cook the raan in a thick-bottomed saucepan on medium flame. Keep the pan covered and turn the meat to ensure both sides absorb enough masalas. It can also be barbecued over slow burning coals or baked in an oven at 150° F. Cook till the meat is done well or as desired. If cooking in an oven, cover with tin foil to prevent drying.

---

[10] Tip: The quantity of papaya paste depends on the meat. For tender meat, 2 tbsp papaya paste is enough. If it is a large meat piece and with more fat, use 3 tbsp. Papaya milk is even more potent. If the milk comes out when the raw papaya is sliced, the slices can be rubbed on the meat.

7. Serve it hot on a dish. Make a salad of onion rings, green chillies and coriander. Put it around the raan. Squeeze half a lemon on it.

Kaleji Curry

Liver and kidney curry.
A family recipe shared by my aunt, Fauzia Khan. She learnt it from her aunt who was (as all Rampuri ladies) very particular about making sure that the curry had no basaind (bad smells).

Ingredients

250 gm liver pieces (kaleji)[11]
250 gm kidney pieces
2 medium-sized onions, finely diced
2 tbsp garlic paste
1 tbsp ginger paste
4–5 crushed garlic cloves
100 gm curd
1/2 tsp turmeric powder
3 tsp coriander powder
2–3 tsp red chilli powder (or as per taste)
100 gm or 4 tbsp refined oil

---

[11] If it is only liver curry, use 1/2 kg liver pieces.

1 tsp dried fenugreek leaves (kasoori methi)
5–6 cloves
2–3 black cardamoms
1 tsp peppercorns
8–9 bay leaves
1 tsp salt (or as per taste)

Method

1. Wash the meat thoroughly. Put it in a deep pan. Add water till it is covered. Add crushed garlic cloves and 5 bay leaves. Boil the meat till it is semi-cooked. Test it with a knife—it should pierce easily. Throw away the water and reserve the meat.

2. Heat the oil and fry the finely diced onions till golden. Add bay leaves, cloves, peppercorns and cardamoms. Fry the liver–kidney in this masala till the water dries up.

3. Add ginger–garlic pastes and fry. Pour in the curd and add coriander, turmeric and chilli powders and continue to fry them. Pour in 1/2 cup of water and leave it on medium heat.

4. When the meat is soft, add dried fenugreek leaves and sauté till the oil separates. The curry should be thick.

5. Garnish the dish with coriander leaves and slit green chillies. Serve it hot.

Eight

Muharram and Grieving

Is waqt sab jahan meri aankhon mein hai siyah,
Logon Khuda ke wastey mujhko batao raah;
Sayyed kidhar tadapta hai, amma kidhar hain aah?
Kis simat hai nabi ke nawasey ki qatalgah?

(Now the whole world lies dark before me,
Oh people! For the sake of Allah, show me the way;
Whence lies the Sayyed (Hazrat Husain) writhing?
Where was the grandson of the Prophet slaughtered?)

—Marsiya by Meer Anees

The princely state of Rampur had a significant minority of Shias[1] whose cultural practices formed a dominant aspect of Rampur's ethos of the time. Nawab Sayed Mohammad Ali Khan (1794) was the first Nawab who reportedly converted

---

[1] The Shias are a sect of Muslims.

to the faith under the influence of Nawab Asif ud daulah of Awadh. This became one of the reasons leading to a coup. The majority of Rampur populace was Sunni[2] Pathans, but the Nawabs had subsequently continued to follow Shiism[3] and its rituals centred on the Imambara prayer hall.

Nawab Sayed Hamid Ali Khan was the first Nawab to publicly practice his faith, a matter which greatly perturbed the British colonists who feared a rebellion by the Sunni populace against the young Nawab. A flurry of letters between the British Agent at Bareilly and his representative at Rampur preserved at the Regional Archives, Allahabad, testify to the political significance of the actions of the Nawab. That Nawab Hamid was able to pull off this radical move speaks volumes of his statesmanship as well as his faith. His successor Nawab Sayed Raza Ali Khan faced political disturbance for appointing Shia officials in his administration.

A night before the holy month of Muharram, the majlis prayer meetings commenced at the Imambara; renowned sozkhwans sang elegaic compositions and maulanas from Awadh narrated the heartrending martyrdom of Prophet Muhammad's grandson, Hazrat Imam Husain, and his followers at the battle of Karbala. It was Nawab Hamid's practice to walk with the procession bearing the zareeh[4] to the Imambara a day before the commencement of Muharram, the month of mourning. He attended all the prayer meetings for

---

[2] The Sunnis are a sect of Muslims.

[3] According to official history of Rampur, all Nawabs since Nawab Sayed Muhammad Ali Khan [ruled 1794], except for Nawab Sayed Kalbe Ali Khan (ruled 1865–1887), were practicing Shias.

[4] A replica of the mausoleum of Imam Husain

the first twelve days of the month and practised abstinence and fasting. On Ashura, the tenth day of Muharram, he walked barefoot and turbanless in a procession to the Karbala burial ground on the outskirts of the town for symbolic burial of the tazia bier of Hazrat Imam Husain. The Nawab carried the alam (the banner of the holy army of Imam Husain) and walked with the male members of the royal family, performing the maatam[5] to the singing of marsiya[6] compositions. The taziyas were borne on the shoulders of mourners; the officials of the state followed the taziya, and the Rampur royal army, the soldiers with their guns lowered, escorted the procession. The participants wore black, some bore alams, and beat their chests to the cry 'Wai Muhammad kushta shud Husain' (Alas, Muhammad, Husain is killed!) All forms of entertainments and festivities were banned during the twelve-day mourning; even the Sunnis didn't celebrate weddings or other occasions during this period. Sunnis also attended the prayer meetings and listened to the narrations; they, however, did not practise the maatam. The 'tabarruq' of three laddus wrapped in a silk kerchief was given to the attendees of the majlis, and langar food was distributed to all. Every evening, a special rose and loban scented milk sherbet was distributed.

On the seventh day of Muharram, a mehndi procession went to the zenana in the fort with beautifully decorated henna platters, flowers, candles and fruits to commemorate Hazrat Qasim and Bibi Fatima's wedding, which was performed during the Karbala campaign—a doomed marriage that lasted

---

[5] A practice of beating chest, or self-flagellation as an expression of grief.
[6] Mourning compositions.

for a day before the final massacre. The majlis on this day was held at the zenana Imambara presided over by Her Highness Begum Rampur. There were prayers and nazar offerings in most households during the first ten days of the month.

The Shia subculture of Rampur, with its elegant traditions and practices emulating Awadh traditions, flourished with the support of the Nawabs. Today, the dwindling community of Shias who had settled in Rampur under the Nawabs still preserves its heritage. The Imambara at Khasbagh Palace is maintained by the members of the royal family who host resplendent, well-attended majlis meetings. The maulana seated on the high podium—silver steps leading up to a small platform with a chair—recounts emotional and evocative narrations. As in Awadh, the traditional chhuri matam[7] is practiced. However, the processions lack the grandeur of the princely times. The Imambaras—inside the qila, as well as at the Khasbagh Palace—have beautiful alam banners displayed on the walls and zareeh contributed by the members of the royal family. The zenana Imambara inside the qila has zareeh set up by the begums of the Nawab, which differ in sizes according to the position of the begum in the harem pecking order.

The unique feature of the zareehs at Rampur are that the replicas are to scale of the shrine of Hazrat Imam Husain in Karbala. My grandfather as the riyasat engineer was deputed by Nawab Sayed Raza Ali Khan to get the exact measurements of the shrine from Karbala. Family lore says he pretended to be a Shia officer of the Nawab while he stayed at Karbala. I

---

[7] Self-flagellation with knives

believe the mission was fraught with danger and Nana Abba had to take the measurements secretly at night. His sketches of the floor plans and elevations became the base for all the zareehs produced at the time. I feel proud when members of the royal family point out Nana Abba's contribution to Rampuri zareehs.

Rare paintings depicting the battle of Karbala and portraits of the Imams are preserved in the Imambara of Khasbagh palace. In an alleged burglary in 1980, some of the golden alams encrusted with precious stones and gold plates were stolen from the Khasbagh Palace.

The khichda is a one-dish meal associated with Muharram in Rampur, though it is now available all year round as street food. The dish is said to have originated post the Karbala massacre when the survivors—mostly women and children and one son of Hazrat Imam Husain—returned to the city of Kufa in Iraq. Unconfirmed oral history says that the people of Kufa cooked a dish from seven types of grains and meat available in their houses to feed the devastated members of Hazrat Imam Husain's family and army.

Harisa, a similar wheat and meat dish, is described in the oldest Arabic cookbooks—*Kitab al-Tabikh* (The Book of Recipes)—written by Saif al-Dawlah Al-Hamdani in tenth-century Syria. Hamdani describes harisa as a speciality made of wheat, beaten into a paste and cooked with meat and spices. Harisa has been a part of Arab, Lebanese, Middle Eastern and Persian cuisine—with differing food stories—which found its way to India via Iran and Afghanistan during the Mughal era. Salma Hussain's translation of *Nuskha e Shahjahani* describes the preparation of harisa with whole wheat and meat, and harisa adas with rice, wheat and pulses cooked with meat. Thus, harisa metamorphosed into the haleem when lentils were added along with beaten wheat at some point in the culinary history of the Indian subcontinent. The Hyderabadi haleem also has lentils, wheat and meat with spices. A chef from Yemen is said to have first prepared the dish in 1930 for the then Nizam of Hyderabad. Subsequently, some Irani hotels started selling it. The ingredients, their proportions and the texture of haleem differ in the subcontinent; the simplicity of the dish lends itself to versatility.

The term khichda, used interchangeably with haleem, is of Indian origin possibly derived from the word khichdi, meaning a mixture. The Rampur khichda has rice, oats, wheat and lentils with meat. The Rampuris scorn any evidence of whole grains in the porridge, prompting the khansamas to advocate the use of mixer-grinders to grind the grains to a paste-like consistency. On the other hand, Shia communities shun the labour-intensive reduction of the dish into a mush. They prefer a grainier texture using seven grains. Sometimes, the meat pieces are blended into the porridge. However, in Rampur, the meat pieces are left whole in the harmonious grain blend and garnished with golden fried onions, ginger juliennes, coriander leaves and green chillies. A dash of vinegar or lemon juice counters the spice with tartness. Indians have succeeded in making a simple, boiled meat porridge opulent by cooking the meat in a spicy curry before adding it into the boiled and mashed grains. Khichda or haleem is also a popular dish during the fasting month of Ramzan in the subcontinent.

Another interesting food story about khichda is centred around Prophet Noah's voyage on the ark. On the tenth day, the ark was caught in a storm. Noah and his family cooked a dish from seven grains and meat. Interestingly, this story was narrated to me by a Sunni gentleman from Bihar. Maybe the Sunni community decided to amalgamate khichda into their gastronomical repertoire by creating another oral history around it. Today, the seven-grain and meat dish is cooked on the Ashura or the tenth day of Muharram—the day corresponding to the day of the Karbala battle and the martyrdom of Imam Husain and his followers. The dish is set in clay bowls and distributed to the mourners. The beauty of the dish is in its simplicity and nutritious content. The mourners break their fast by eating khichda.

Maleeda, made of flatbread pounded into a grainy powder and sweetened with sugar or jaggery, is also a snack associated with Muharram. It is a lot like Gujarati and Rajasthani churma. Since eating paan is also not allowed during the mourning period, muslin pouches with dhaniya-gota—a mixture of roasted almonds, coriander seeds, coconut, aniseed and betel nuts—are distributed in the majlis as mouth freshners. Both sects fast on the ninth and tenth day of Muharram.

Growing up in a Sunni household, we had our own Muharram traditions to give due respect to the martyrs. Nani Amma, always a great one for fatiha, prayed over doodh sherbet (milk sherbet) made of watered-down milk, sugar, cardamom and rose water. It was distributed to all the children and the families of the servants living in the outhouses. I loved the doodh sherbet, but I didn't know it was supposed to be smoked with oudh incense. Perhaps it was too tedious a process, so we had the simple rose-scented milk sherbet. During winter Muharrams, we substituted the doodh sherbet with clove-flavoured chai cooked over slow fire with lots of milk. We went to a majlis on the seventh day of Muharram to my father's Shia relatives and on the day of Ashura, my mother gathered the children around her and read the events of the Karbala battle from a green book. The aunts would also listen in and soon there would be cathartic crying. 'The green book is out,' the boys would whisper and run away to play. So, it was mostly us, the girls, listening to the story and comforting our mothers. Begum Jahanara Habibullah, who also belonged to a Sunni family reminisces of a similar practice of reading the *Shahadatnama*—the narrative on the martyrdom of Imam Husain and his followers—by her mother. Out of respect for the martyrs, we were forbidden from watching TV or listening to songs during the ten-day mourning period. Going for a movie was inconceivable, and we waited desperately for the ten-day ban to end. It was after we grew up that we realized the immensity of the tragedy, which consume the Muslims with grief year after year.

Khichda

Niggo baji, our lady cook at my grandparents' house, prepares the best khichda. When we visit there, this one-dish meal is definitely on the food itinerary. Her proportions are slightly different from the Rampur khichda proportions set down below.

Ingredients

250 gm barley (jau)
250 gm broken wheat
250 gm chana dal
100 gm white urad dal
100 gm arhar dal
100 gm red split masoor dal
100 gm rice
1 1/2 kg meat
3 large onions, finely diced
4 tbsp ginger–garlic paste
4 tbsp onion paste
1 1/2 tbsp turmeric powder
1 1/2 tbsp red chilli powder or to taste
6 tsp coriander powder
1 cup ghee, refined oil or mustard oil
4 bay leaves
5 black cardamoms
5 cloves
5 green cardamoms
4 tsp garam masala powder
1 tsp aromatic powder
1 tsp garam masala powder
Salt to taste

For the garnish

2 onions, golden fried
3 inch piece of ginger, julienned

5-6 green chillies, cut fine

2 bunches of coriander leaves

2-3 lemons, cut into wedges

Method

1. Soak barley, wheat, chana dal and urad dal (separately) overnight.

2. In a pressure cooker, boil barley and wheat with 1 tsp salt, 1 tsp turmeric powder, 1/2 tsp chilli powder and 2 cups of water. The grains should be soft and mashable. Set it aside and mash.

3. In a separate cooker (or the same cooker after its empty) pressure cook chana dal with 1 tsp salt, 1 tsp turmeric powder, 1/2 tsp chilli powder and 1 cup of water. When it is soft, add the rest of the lentils and rice. Add 1/2 cup water and cook.

4. When these are done, add the barley and wheat mix and cool. Every dal takes different amount of time to cook so we have to cook them separately.

5. In a pan, heat the ghee or refined oil (or mustard oil but heat it till the smell evaporates); fry the onions till they are golden. Drain them and put them on a kitchen tissue.

6. Add the meat, whole spices and bay leaves, and fry. Add ginger, garlic and onion pastes and sauté. Add remaining turmeric, coriander and chilli powders. Continue to sauté till the masalas are done and the oil separates. Add 1 cup of water and pressure cook till the meat is tender. Add half the fried and hand-crushed onions.

7. Mix the dals well. They should have a thick, homogenous consistency. If required, blend them in a mixer-grinder.

8. Add the lentils to the meat and boil. Mix them thoroughly. Add the garam masala and aromatic powder.
9. Garnish it and serve it hot. Keep extra garnish on the side with lemon wedges. Some people eat khichda with a dash of red vinegar or curd.

Maleeda

We often make maleeda out of makka or bajra roti sweetened with jaggery. This is my favourite because it has a unique texture and taste.

Ingredients

2 crisp parathas (freshly made or leftover)/makka roti/bajra roti
1 tbsp ghee
10—15 almonds
10—15 raisins
Half a coconut, roughly grated
2—3 tsp powdered sugar or gur
1 tsp green cardamom powder

Method

1. Pound the roti/paratha or put these through a mixer-grinder.

2. In a pan, heat the ghee and fry the almonds and raisins on low heat. Switch off the flame and sauté the coconut. Cool them and grind them in a mixer-grinder.
3. Add to roti/paratha powder.
4. Add sugar/jaggery and cardamom powder.
5. Serve it hot or at room temperature.

Nine

Nauroz Beginnings and Predictions

My grandfather, Zaigham Husain, would seat my sister and me in his room and speak of Muharram rituals, cry listening to mournful marsiyas and exalt the wonderful spread of sweetmeats on Nauroz. Sitting on his prickly, woollen blanket, we found his crying on the martyrdom of Hazrat Imam Husain unreal, but we were caught up with fabled Nauroz dishes, colours and celebrations. Even as little girls, we knew that it was impossible to celebrate Nauroz in our house because our mother was a staunch Sunni Muslim and Papa had given up his Shia religious practices when he got married, much to our grandfather's angst. But Dada, valiantly trying to bring us back to the true faith, gave us an alternate Shia reality that our lives could slip into. He even gave us Shia names. Mine was Narjis, and as I was born on Nauroz, it became my favourite imaginary festival, which I 'celebrated' in the persona of the elegant Narjis, with my younger sister, in her Shia identity of Shirin, assisting me in laying out the sweets and welcoming the new year. Nauroz always fascinated me because it fell on my birthday and made me feel like a very special child.

Nauroz (lit. New Day) is celebrated on the 20 or 21 March as the sun enters into Aries, marking the beginning of the Persian New Year. An ancient Iranian spring festival, Nauroz was integrated into Islam particularly into the Shia sect of Islam. Nauroz and Mehregan (harvest festival) were the two Persian festivals marking the summer and winter solstices, respectively. Imam Jafar, the sixth Imam or religious leader of the Shias, had instructed special prayers and fasts on Nauroz. Thus, a traditional spring festival got integrated in the socio-cultural milieu with religious overtones. It heralds new beginnings, hope for the new year and spiritual regeneration with prayers recited over fruits and grains. The Shia communities in Iran, Iraq, Afghanistan and Turkey celebrate it with rich symbolism of life in the form of elaborately decorated display of mirrors, newly sprouted wheat, candles, sweets and fruits. On the thirteen day of the new year, the newly sprouted green is floated away in a natural body of water to release the old and welcome the new. Nauroz is also celebrated by the Zoroastrians all over the world as the beginning of a new year.

According to Shia oral tradition and as per narration from Imam Musa Khadim (AS), the archangel Gabriel appeared before Prophet Muhammad for the first time on Nauroz; it is also said to be the day when Prophet Abraham entered the house of God, the Kaaba, to break the idols thus declaring the new religion of Islam. Imam Sadiq reportedly said, 'With the beginning of Farvardin, (the first month of the Persian solar Hijri calendar which begins with Nauroz) humans were created, and this day is an auspicious day for praying to seek dreams, to visit the nobles, acquire knowledge, marry, travel and do good business. In this blessed day the sick will be cured, babies will be born hassle-free and sustenance will increase.' During the Safavid rule in Iran, Nauroz was adopted into the Islamic culture. Seven symbolic items, the haft seen, whose name begin with the sibilant 'seen' alphabet, are prepared and set on the ceremonial table for the prayers. Certain passages from the holy Quran are read out as part of the observances.

In Rampur, the credit of celebrating this ancient festival with great festivity goes to Nawab Sayed Hamid Ali Khan. Nawab Hamid and the male members of the royal family and the court attended the special prayers recited by the maulvi. New fruits, sweetmeats and grains were kept in silver qaabs or serving dishes. At the centre of the dining table, seven ground grains or grist were displayed in silver dishes. A rose was floated on water in a silver bowl. The tradition of floating a rose in water possibly has its roots in the subcontinent. It is probable that the earlier Nawabs as followers of Shiism also celebrated Nauroz.

Bilquis Jahan Begum, in her unpublished diary, *Darbar e Rampur*, penned her uncle's eyewitness account of an incident at Nauroz celebration. Nawab Hamid stood before the Nauroz spread and prayed to Hazrat Ali[1] to accept the offering and grant peace and prosperity to his domain. He then left the room and asked the gathering to leave as well, and the door was locked for some time. When they re-entered, they found that the ground grain had finger marks on it, as if someone

---

[1] Hazrat Ali was the cousin and son-in-law of Prophet Muhammad (SAW) and the fourth caliph of Islam.

had picked up the flour. This was a sign that the offering was accepted by Hazrat Ali himself.

Nawab Sayed Hamid Ali Khan, as all the Nawabs of Rampur, was tolerant towards other religions and his begums were free to follow their own faiths, but the court etiquettes enforced by the Nawab through his lady guards, the Daroghans, made it incumbent upon them to give due respect to Shia rituals. Some of his begums converted to Shiism to please the Nawab. One of the begums belonged to a Sunni Pathan family. Her father was among the chief critics of the Nawab's Shia faith and was often reported voicing his censure indiscreetly. The Nawab promptly sent a proposal to marry his daughter. The new begum, given the title of Munawwar Dulhan Begum, entered the zenana and was given a mahalsara (palace) guarded by the inimitable Daroghan and a posse of eunuchs and female guards. The Begum followed her Sunni faith and employed Sayyid ladies, descendants of Prophet Muhammad, to perform the rituals on her behalf.

The Nawab often organized various festivities in the zenana attended by his twenty-two begums, resplendent in their long farshi skirts, with their royal jewels on display. One incident about Nauroz celebration is described by Bilquis Jahan Begum in *Darbar e Rampur* which was narrated to her by her aunt, a Daroghan in the zenana. Nawab Hamid played colours on Nauroz at the Shahenshah Manzil, a palace in the zenana. On one such Nauroz, all the ladies of the harem— his wives and female relatives—dressed in white churidar-kameez and armed with silver pistons were ready to play with Nawab Hamid. The Shahenshah Manzil had beautiful lawns

edged with fruit trees and large tanks for watering the area.
A tank in the mahal was filled with coloured water—the hue
was prescribed by the clerics in Iran as the Nauroz colour of
the year. The Nawab entered, dressed in a white angarkha and
churidar. On his head, he wore the famous 'Hamid cap'—a
precursor to the Gandhi cap. He was the only male present
at the celebration. A begum from Lucknow was given the
honour of spraying the colour first on the pristine white dress
of the Nawab. Everyone then rushed to fill their pistons with
colour and played with gay abandon.

Suddenly, the Nawab paused and asked, 'Where is
Munawwar Begum?' The Daroghan salaamed and said, 'Sarkar,
she is unwell and sends her excuses.' The Nawab understood
that the haughty Begum did not want to participate in the
celebration of a Shia festival. He immediately asked the female
guards to escort the Begum to Shahenshah Mahal. The guards
who went to call Munawwar Begum returned empty-handed
and reported that the Begum was resting.

'Wake her up and bring her here!' he thundered and sent
them back again to the Begum's residence.

Astounded at Munawwar Begum's audacity, the other
begums paused their play, frozen into immobility at the
Nawab's rage. He was known to be unforgiving and vindictive
in his fury. The guards returned and reported that the Begum
was awake but had refused to come. By now the Nawab was
beside himself with anger at the blatant defiance.

'Bring the Begum with the bed she is lying on!' he
commanded.

The maids and guards ran back, tried to remonstrate
with Begum Munawwar, told her about the command of the

Nawab, but the Begum covered herself with her sequinned coverlet and held on to the side of the bed, stubbornly refusing to comply. The female guards were helpless. They carried the recalcitrant Begum lying on her bed to Shahenshah Manzil, which was practically adjacent to her residence and set her down in the garden. The Nawab towered over the prone Begum, and the revellers, drenched in colours, watched agog.

'Throw her in the tank along with her bed!' shouted the Nawab and stormed out of the palace.

The female guards obeyed the order, and the Begum was completely immersed in the water along with her bed. The other wives looked on, no doubt enjoying the fall of the proud Begum. Munawwar Begum, drenched and humiliated, had to be fished out of the pool and escorted back to her residence.

It is said that she blamed the Lucknow begums for her humiliation and never spoke to them again. There is hardly any reference to Munawwar Begum after this incident. My guess is that she relented and made up with her husband. She probably found favour with the Nawab again because Nawab Hamid gave his third son, from another begum, to the childless Munawwar Begum. Bilquis Jahan Begum writes that the Nawab was kind and caring towards her though he detested her lofty attitude towards the other begums. After Nawab Hamid's death, some begums went to live with their relatives and were given pension, but Munawwar Begum lived at the zenana section of Khasbagh Palace along with the rest of the Nawab's widows. They were well looked after by their stepson and the new Nawab—Nawab Sayed Raza Ali Khan. They attended all official functions, seated together, their power skirmishes forgotten. Old-timers say there were about twenty of them dressed in white ghararas and chiffon dupattas. Everyone had to pay their respects to them immediately after entering the mehfil.

'My back would hurt bowing and salaaming to the whole row of them,' an old aunt told me.

Today, Nauroz is celebrated in Rampur by the Shia Muslims in their homes and Imambaras, toned down drastically from the earlier pomp. It is regarded as more of a womanly affair. The time and colour of the festival are decided by Iranian clerics.

A few years ago, I visited a Shia friend's home to witness the festival; I was dressed in red, the colour of Nauroz that year. Spread out on the floor rug were various foods (kababs, pulao, qorma, boiled eggs), grains (sattu), fruits (apples, oranges, bananas) and sweets. The declared colour of sweets was white, so there were milk-based sweetmeats as well as orange zarda. There were haft-seen or seven foods beginning with the 'seen' alphabet—sabzeh (wheat saplings), seer (garlic), seb (apple), sirkeh (vinegar) etc. For convenience, people stick to sweets and the new fruit of the season, symbolizing spring.

In a crystal bowl, at the centre of the spread, was a red rose floating on water. It is said that if the rose is put in the water at the exact time of the equinox or the time when the sun enters Aries, it will start floating in a circular path. The lady of the house had inscribed Arabic prayers for prosperity and protection from the evil eye on three white ceramic plates with a reed pen dipped in saffron water. The 'panja' (hand) emblem of Hazrat Ali and the banners of Imam Jafar occupied a prominent position on a table with red mannat threads representing the prayers of the family members. At the prescribed time, when the sun entered Aries, red and green candles were lit with a single white candle and the members of the family stood up to recite the prayers.

'The rose moves on its own in the centre and around the bowl if our wishes are granted. But for the past three years, it hasn't stirred. I have asked the others—the rose hasn't moved in any of the houses. It is a bad time for Muslims all over the world,' said our hostess.

We partook of the prayed-over food; a Sayyed lady took the first serving. A bamboo fan was dipped in holy water, and the water was sprinkled over us and in all corners of the house. Later, the saffron writing was washed into the rose bowl and the water was sprinkled in all corners of the house to ward off the evil eye.

The year when the pandemic first engulfed us, the unthinkable happened. Black was declared as Nauroz colour. It was not a colour, but a lack thereof. Even the oldest members of the community did not remember black being the prescribed Nauroz colour; for how can the colour of mourning symbolize the colour of new beginnings? The time for the sun to move into Aries that year was 3.07 p.m. on 20 March. As if the colour of Nauroz wasn't portent enough, the black rose floating in the bowl of water didn't move at all.

Ten

The Melody of Charbait Barsati

Aaya barsat ka mausam mera larjey hai jiya
Piya pardes mein hain . . .
Sakht ghabrayi hoon chunri ko doon main aag laga,
Piya pardes mein hain.

(The monsoon season is bursting upon us
My heart is a-tremble, my lover is away . . .
My anxiety increases every moment,
I want to burn my colourful scarf,
My lover. is away.)
A traditional Barsati song of Rampur.

From the veranda, we would watch the rains lashing our
courtyard, and all of us—the aunts, cousins, uncles and my
Nani Amma—sang the simple tune. We, girls, sniggered at
the silly, romantic heroine of the song pining for her beloved.
One of us would spontaneously mime the volatile emotions of

the lovelorn heroine—pretending to burn up the scarf, calling the 'Brahman' for palm reading, making henna patterns—and the others would burst into riotous laughter. Nani Amma would frown at us for spoiling the song. While researching Rampur culture, I realized that the simple song was actually a charbait—a quatrain composition of four-line stanzas, traditionally sung by the Pathans to the accompaniment of the tambourine. Over centuries, these compositions documented battles fought, celebrated heroes, or spoke of love, loss and seasons; the linguistic metamorphosis from Pashto to Urdu and Hindvi spoke of the assimilation of the Pathan ethos into Indian culture. Composed by Nawabs, nobility and poets, charbaits became songs of ordinary farmers and labourers in mohallas and street corners after a hard day's labour. Nawab Sayed Hamid Ali Khan, Nawab Sayed Raza Ali Khan and his wife, Raffat Zamani Begum, penned charbaits incorporating Hindvi and Urdu words—a reflection of the changing notes of the spoken language.

The Pathans migrating from the cool climes of Swat and Roh highlands passionately rejoiced in the relief of monsoons. Monsoon and love became the most popular themes of charbait as the Pathans became enamoured with the rains and celebrated monsoons with food and songs. The Nawabs organized charbait competitions till the 1960s and supported the local talent. There must be several compositions by women in the zenana tracing the meters of the quatrain with their emotions. These songs, sung briefly, were lost after one or two generations. My Nani Amma wrote barsatis and ghazals in a diary and would sometimes sit trying to set them to simple, mournful tunes. I searched vainly for the diary

with its curving Urdu script; we have also forgotten her lines
of loneliness and despair trailing her battle with depression.
Nani Amma's favourite barsati charbait featuring the hyper-
emotional heroine was composed by Nawab Sayed Raza Ali
Khan in the most passionate tradition of charbait—a perfect
mirror of a Pathan persona—straightforward and emotive.

Even today, the Rampuris, with their latent agrarian
consciousness, engage intensely with the monsoons. There is a
sub-culture of romantic charbait songs and monsoon fare that
comes into play as the first purple, pregnant clouds congeal
in the sky. Sawanis (monsoon feasts) are organized in mango
orchards that edge the city, with swings for ladies and children,
soulful barsati songs, fried treats and freshly plucked mangoes
in iced buckets. Those who do not have the luxury of strolling
in mango orchards, cook monsoon treats at home.

Historical records of traditional feasts and soirees held
in orchards go back to the mid-nineteenth century during
the time of Nawab Sayed Kalbe Ali Khan. Jashn e Benazir
or Mela Benazir was held in spring every year in the mango
orchards of Benazir Palace, the summer palace of the Nawab.
The *Musaddas e Tahniyat e Jashn e Benazir* (Felicitation for the
Incomparable Festival), written in 1867–1868 by Mir Yar Ali
Jan Sahib Rekhtigo (1818–1886) eloquently describes the
scenes of the mela.[1] The poets, dastango (storytellers), tawaifs,
courtesans, dancers and singers, performing for commoners
and kings were invited from Delhi, Agra, Lucknow and
Calcutta. The unrefined, two-dimensional paintings of the

---

[1] Mir Yar Ali 'Jan Sahib', *The Incomparable Festival* (A masterpiece of Indo-
Islamic literary). Trans. Shad Naved; Ed Dr Razak Khan. New Delhi:
Penguin Random House India, 2021.

mela in Jan Sahib's compilation depict famous courtesans of the time dressed in colourful, trailing farshi skirts, revealing blouses, transparent dupatta veils titillatingly covering their breasts, flaunting high-coiffed hair—daring, brazen and free. He writes of dastangos like Amba Prasad, Ali Hakim, Ahmad Ali and Qasim Ali telling their tales till late at night and the Begums listening from behind the screen. It was here that the poet Dagh Dehlvi met the great love of his life, Munni Bai Hijab Kalkatteywali. The fair would culminate in a display of fireworks and a procession to the Qadam Sharif cenotaph, where the foot impression of the Prophet, brought from Mecca by Nawab Sayed Kalbe Ali Khan, was housed in an octagonal structure.

Sawanis were traditionally celebrated for the newlyweds in old Rampur households. Her Highness Raffat Zamani Begum wrote to her sister Begum Jahanara Habibullah describing the sawani celebrated in her honour at the Benazir Palace orchards. The account is quoted by Begum Jahanara in her memoir. The zenana section of the palace was cordoned off with tented walls to shield the ladies observing purdah. There were swings on the mango trees and tents with takhts on which the begums lounged, enjoying the monsoon. Young voices rose in raag malhaar songs. Elaborate dishes were set out on dastarkhwans. Raffat Zamani Begum wore her special green ensemble from Banaras, jootis with golden bells and the traditional red and green bangles. A swing with a silver seat was set up in the portico of the zenana palace. The crown prince, Raza Ali Khan and his bride, Raffat Zamani Begum, sat on the swing, the Bismillah prayer was recited, and Nawab Sayed Hamid Ali Khan threw hundred-and-one gold asharfis over the young couple as nichhawar to ward off the evil eye. The other relatives also threw asharfis over the bride and groom. Nawab Sayed Hamid Ali Khan was given a cord to pull at and set the swing in motion as the singer sang a composition by the Nawab:

> *Aaj dulhan ko johoola jhulayen*
>   *Kali, kali ghata ghir ghir ayen*

> (Today our bride swings on the jhoola
>   As monsoon clouds gather around.)

Even today, sawani gifts are sent to the bride-to-be's house by her in-laws and to the married daughters by their parents. My sister-in-law sent the sawani—a green dress, green and red bangles, andarsey, pattey, poori—to her son's fiancée.

'She is looking healthier after eating my pattey–poori,' smiled my sister-in-law. The girl was too thin for my hefty nephew, and my sister-in-law was often teased about it, much to her chagrin.

Sawan is also the month when the married daughters come to their paternal homes to enjoy the rains with their sisters and extended families. It coincides with the summer break at school, so the house is packed with daughters and grandchildren. It used to be an annual family time at my grandmother's house too.

My favourite monsoon dish is pattey made of arvi or colocasia leaves rolled with spiced chickpea flour batter, steamed, cut into pinwheels and deep fried. I love the crunchy pattey. I call it a snack rather than a meal because I don't like eating them with pooris, but I have never cooked pattey or watched them being made. The description of the cooking procedure is quite complicated, so I usually beg my sister-in-law to make some for me. This year, because of the COVID scare and the lockdown, I didn't receive my favourite snack and was forced to attempt to cook it. Also, as I was writing about it, I thought it would be better to cook it first.

I called up the sister-in-law and jotted down the spices to put into the besan and the procedure. I managed to slather the besan on layers of colocasia leaves, roll them up and steam them in an improvised steamer. My instructress assumed that I would know that the sides of the roll had to be tucked in to prevent the batter from oozing out. It got messy during the steaming, but I managed to cut the pinwheels and fry them to a crispy brown. Some people also put it into a thin gravy and serve it as a curry.

As arvi or colocasia leaves are a local produce, the dish is prepared in all communities of Rampur. It is similar to Gujarati paatra and Marathi lavingya. Since no mention of the dish is found in the historical writings from the princely era, I suspect the dish was a local dish, which was adapted into the culinary and cultural milieu of Rampur.

The final flourish at all monsoon feasts is the piping hot, sweet andarsey brought from the local halwai. Andarsey, the traditional monsoon sweet, is an Epicurean delight with a crunchy, reddish-gold crust, freckled with crisp sesame seeds, and fluffy, grainy, moist insides. The earthiness of rice flour is balanced with the nutty flavour of the sesame seeds. It is prepared from rice flour, ghee and sugar batter shaped into flat cakes—sometimes with a hole at the centre—and deep fried.

The conventional cooking wisdom dictates that the rice flour should be kneaded with rainwater to make it extra spongy. Perhaps, rainwater containing bicarbonates helped the dough to rise. So, though some halwais prepare it throughout the year, it is believed that the true masters only start off the monsoon sweet after the first monsoon showers have brought down the dust and the rainwater is pure enough for use.

No monsoon is complete without the delectable indulgence of Mumtaz Bhai's andarsey. Other halwais fry the fritters all year around but people wait for Mumtaz Bhai to begin frying the sweet and declare the season open. Mumtaz Bhai, the founder of the iconic shop, is of course long dead and his grandson claims that the recipe has been handed down through generations from his ancestors who worked in the Nawab's kitchens. The Rampuris scoff at the claim—nearly every khansama professes descent from the line of royal chefs.

Mumtaz Bhai's shop with its grimy awning, sooty walls and faded sign is an anathema to its glorious repute. It has not expanded or modernized since its inception which, he says, dates to right after the merger of Rampur State into Indian Union in 1949. There must have been at least three generations of Mumtaz Bhai since the 1950s, all referred to by the name of the founder, in greasy kurta pyjama, faces glistening from the heat of the fire, briskly frying andarsey and other sweets.

The current 'Mumtaz Bhai' starts frying the fritters around five in the evening, his large kadhai—blackened with decades of grease—brims with ghee and andarsey discs. He is soon surrounded by customers, pulled in by the sweet aroma, watching the andarsey acquire a deep golden hue. There is a directness to the experience of watching the andarsey being fried at the shop and the casual informality of the newspaper packets bearing the sweets.

Lining up for andarsey is a male domain, but I cover my head with a dupatta, brave the curious stares, try to slot myself in and take a place in the expectant circle. I greet Mumtaz Bhai, tell him that I have heard so much about his andarsey that I had to come myself to see him make it.

He smiles, mopping his face, and asks, 'Bibi, where are you from?'

I have to cite ancestral and mohalla references since all introductions here begin from grandparents or even great-grandparents.

'Do you still use rainwater?' I ask. I hear someone whisper, 'Journalist'.

'No, no. Rainwater is so dirty now. We use soda,' Mumtaz Bhai laughs. 'The secret is our honesty. Most roadside shops fry andarsey in low quality oil which leaves an aftertaste. We use only ghee.'

I start munching from the greasy paper packet as soon as I get on to the rickshaw. The sweet is stippled with melon seeds instead of sesame seeds but the flavour is sacrosanct; or so I thought.

'They don't taste the same anymore. There was a subtle caramel flavour that I miss.' My mother has the most perceptive taste buds, and I scurry to the Raza Library in search of the missing ingredient.

Several Persian and Urdu manuscripts and cookbooks on Indo-Persian, Mughal, Awadhi and Rampur cuisine dating late-nineteenth century describe the process of preparing

andarsey in some detail. A recipe of 'andarsa' is also found
in the seventeenth century *Nuskha e Shahjahani*. As per a
manuscript attributed to Nawab Sayed Kalbe Ali Khan of
Rampur, rice was soaked overnight and ground to a fine
paste. It was then kneaded with ghee and sugar syrup—
possibly unrefined sugar called qand—to prepare the pastry.
So, the unrefined sugar, cooked to a thick syrup, must have
contributed to the caramel taste that Mamma remembers
from her childhood. One recipe advocates mixing some curd
to make the dough rise. I guess soda was not easily available or
used in Indian cooking at that time.

On my way back from the library, I ask a frantically busy
Mumtaz Bhai Jr about the sugar syrup. He says he just puts in
powdered sugar into the rice flour with some ghee and soda
powder. The rice is not soaked overnight any more since rice
flour is readily available. Somewhere we abridged the process,
substituted the ingredients and forgot the essence of the dish.

'Don't bother. No one eats andarsey anymore. Children
prefer ice creams!', says Mamma.

Andarsey sweet is more popular in the old city area. It was
an important part of our monsoon celebrations at Aligarh.
The sweets came in cheap, gruesome pink cardboard boxes
and looked like shrivelled disks, dotted with sesame seeds—
an unappetizing sight that hardly merited any gastronomic
yearning. Yet my Nani Amma and gaggle of aunts, congregating
for the summer break with their brood, would send fervent
demands for Mumtaz Bhai's andarsey to be sent post-haste
from Rampur along with the essential monsoon paraphernalia.
The requirement included succulent langdas, bright green and
red kacchi bangles for the married daughters and daughters-

in-law and hand-dyed, crinkled cotton chunris for all girls. The andarsey, lovingly refried and resurrected to its juicy crispness, was served at the barsati singing sessions as we watched the rains pulsate on the brick courtyard.

The antecedents of andarsey cannot be determined. It is called 'andarsey' only in the north Indian Rohilla belt and Pakistan. The Sufi saint Bulley Shah's shrine in Kasur near Lahore is famous for several types of andarsey. It is generally called 'anarsa' or 'adhirasa'—a traditional festival sweet prepared during Diwali all over the country. The recipe is simple and quite similar everywhere with little variations; some use jaggery instead of sugar. On Diwali, it makes sense to have andarsey or anarsa because of the rice harvest but the craving for andarsey while watching the burst of monsoon, is a cultural response. Lucknow and Jaipur have a similar tradition of monsoon anarsa, which raises doubts about the Rampur oral tradition that andarsey sweet was brought in by the Pathans from Afghanistan. Maybe it was a traditional Indian harvest sweet which was incorporated into the monsoon food culture of the region.

Andarsey are rarely made at home in Rampur and we wait for our crunchy supplies from the halwais. Mumtaz Bhai Jr started frying andarsey rather late this year because of the delayed monsoons even though the ingredients have nothing to do with the rains anymore. But there is a time for everything here and pleasures of the tongue dictate an expectant wait for the fullness of time and abundant rains.

Dr Sofia and Dr Mehmood host a sawani at their farm every year. We gorge on freshly fried andarsey as we watch the mango pluckers shimmy up the trees to pluck the langdas—

plumped up and sweetened by the rains—and try to sing the simple lilting barsati charbaits, composed by Nawab Sayed Raza Ali Khan, laughing all the while at the quaint, ever-pining heroine.

Hai ye sawan ki ghata hirday pe chayi jaaye hai,
ae sakhi aisey samay piya bina jiya ghabraye hai . . .

(O friend, the dark monsoon clouds gather around my tumultuous heart,
At such a time, I'm filled with longing for my beloved.)

Ultimately, we end up singing movie songs from the rain drenched lovers genre.

Pattey

Colocasia rolls are sometimes steamed and frozen to last the season. My aunt Shagufta Khan, who passed away during COVID, used to prepare mint leaf rolls—a painstaking process—in a similar fashion and send to me every year.

Ingredients

250 gm chickpea flour
250 gm large colocasia leaves

Mustard oil for shallow frying
1 tsp garlic paste
1 tsp ginger paste
1 tsp turmeric
1–2 tsp red chilli powder (or as per taste)
1/2 tsp ajwain (carom seeds)
1 lemon juice or 1 tsp amchur powder
1 1/2 tsp salt (more than usual salt is required)

Method

1. Make a thick paste of chickpea flour (besan) with ginger-garlic pastes, turmeric powder, salt, carom seeds, chilli powder and lemon juice.
2. Prepare the leaves by washing and trimming the thick central stem.
3. Take one leaf and smear the besan paste on its inner side. Put another leaf on top and smear some more besan.
4. Roll them up, tightly tucking in the sides. Make 2 or 3 such rolls.
5. Take 1 litre of water in a saucepan. Fit a sieve on top. Put the rolls on the sieve, cover them and steam for 1/2 hour. Or use a steamer.
6. When the rolls cool down, cut into 5 cm discs and shallow fry till they are crisp.
7. Serve them hot with chutney and puri.

Andarsey

These are surprisingly easy to make at home but there is a charm to sending someone to fetch them after a fresh bout of rains.

Ingredients

1 1/2 cup rice flour
1/2 cup semolina
1 1/2 cup sugar (or jaggery)
1/2 tsp baking powder
1/2 tsp green cardamom powder (optional)
2 tbsp ghee
1 cup sesame seeds
3/4 cup water
Refined oil or ghee for deep frying

Method

1. Put the sugar or jaggery in water and cook it till it dissolves. Set it aside to cool.
2. In a bowl, mix all the dry ingredients. Add the ghee and mix with hand to make it look like breadcrumbs.
3. Knead the crumbs with sugar water.
4. Set it aside for 1 hour.
5. Take little portions of the dough, shape them into thick discs or little balls and roll them in the sesame seeds.
6. Heat the oil in a deep kadhai. Fry one and check if it is done till its core. Fry the rest on low heat till they turn golden.
7. Serve them hot or store in airtight jars.

Eleven

The Royal Tables and the Comfort of Daily Foods

Nawab Sayed Hamid Ali Khan was considered the connoisseur and epicure of his age. Nawab Hosh Yaar Jung Bilgrami, who was a courtier at Nawab Hamid's durbar for ten years, describes the grand culinary repertoire of Rampur cuisine at its zenith in his work *Mashahidaat*. At Nawab Hamid's banquets, 700 to 800 guests were served nearly 200 dishes from cuisines around the world—Indian, Persian, Turkish, English and Continental— and the guests, egged on by the Nawab, a perfect host, would get exhausted eating the delicious fare. Bilgrami further writes that the British, Iranian and Turkish guests would set aside their bland cuisines and partake of Rampur fare offered to them. The Nawab employed 150 khansamas in three main kitchens— the Indian kitchen, the English kitchen and the sweetmeat kitchen[1]—and each khansama specialized in only one dish.

---

[1] Oral history contradicts this slightly in adding a rice kitchen to the paraphernalia.

Bilgrami writes, 'Such cooks could not be found in the kitchens of the Mughal emperors or in Turkey and Egypt.' The Nawab's kitchens were bare of any red chillies or black pepper, according to Bilgrami. Serving food became a performance, an element of gastrodiplomacy, and the Nawab became a renowned food connoisseur hosting the most magnificent tables.

The Nawab himself ate Indian food once a day, supervised by the royal hakims. He drank the water collected during monsoons, which was preserved in silver vessels. He also drank iced watermelon juice throughout the year.

Rampur court was known for its legendary hospitality. The State guests stayed in the royal guesthouse palaces and were served the *khaasey ka khaana* or special fare which consisted of mutton qorma, kababs, qaliya, sheermaal (sweet flat bread) and a rice dish. Paan, milk, dry fruits, seasonal fruits and other essential groceries were sent daily to the guesthouse. If a guest chose to stay at a friend's place, his food sent from the royal kitchens would suffice for an entire family. The State guests lived at the palace for years. The Nawab even sent some stipend to their homes for the upkeep of their families.

Mehrunnisa Begum narrates an incident in which a hapless guest was made to sample a spoonful each of the 200 dishes by Nawab Hamid—thirty chicken dishes, twenty-five meat dishes, fifty lentil dishes, ten pulaos and several other delicacies. After two and a half hours of eating, the guest had to summon the physician; he was administered ENO salts. Later he remarked that the banquet nearly killed him![2]

---

[2] Mehrunissa Khan, *An Extraordinary Life: Princess Mehrunissa of Rampur.* Noida: Blue Leaf, 2006.

Though his successor, Nawab Sayed Raza Ali Khan, reduced the number of cooks to thirty, the grand journey of the cuisine continued. Jahanara Begum's memoir of Nawab Sayed Raza Ali Khan's era highlights a detailed account of the dishes served at the royal tables in a separate section titled 'The Royal Tables at the Court of Rampur'. The qormas and qaliyas are common to most Indian Muslim cuisines as are the styles of pulaos and kababs, but some remarkable variations of these dishes are mentioned in the book along with some novel preparations. The dumpukht pulao with a whole chicken, quail, partridge or leg of mutton was a Rampuri speciality, as was the kundan qaliya with its light, saffron-flavoured gravy. Ratan qaliya was cooked like the kundan qaliya with the addition of meat balls along with mutton and chicken pieces and a garnish of boiled egg yolks. The Rampuri shabdegh had slow-cooked gravy with meatballs, mutton pieces and turnips. Mutanjan was sweet and savoury rice—sweet gulab jamuns and savoury meatballs—that used sugar four times the weight of rice. Princess Naghat Abedi disclosed that the meatballs were stuffed with dry fruits and dipped in sweet syrup. She loved the nursery sweets, especially tiny fruit baskets—each basket an individual serving—shaped from toffee caramel filled with fruit salad in cream. Muneeza Shamsie recalls a similar treat prepared by her Rampuri khansama in Karachi.

The stylized presentations of sweet rice were extraordinary—grapes contrived out of petha garnished the grape pulao, pomegranate seeds made from sugar and edible colour were scattered on anar (pomegranate) pulao and a life-sized pineapple sat atop the anannas (pineapple) pulao dish. The kabab uroos e behri was a two-feet-long fish kabab, which resembled a fish—with scales, face and tongue—an ingenious presentation by the skilled khansamas. The halwa sohan was, and still is, a Rampur speciality made of samnak, wheat germ flour, and has Persian–Afghan roots. Some of the other sweets served at the royal tables have been mentioned earlier. Most of these dishes were forgotten in the years following the abolition of privy purses and the disbanding of the royal khansamas.

It wouldn't be an exaggeration to say that on any day if one dined with Nawab Sayed Raza Ali Khan or his son, Nawab Sayed Murtaza Ali Khan, aloo gosht (potato and meat curry) would grace the table. It was a subaltern dish which was a favourite of the Nawabs. Aloo gosht was cooked in an ordinary household; the addition of potatoes made the meat curry go a long way. In my family, aloo gosht was called ghalley ka khana—a dish cooked for the large number of servants in rambling old kothis. The curry was vermilion-red with a layer of turmeric-coloured oil on top, lightly spiced but heavy on red chillies. It was a thin curry—somewhere between watery and thick, an undefinable consistency, almost as if it had been put through a sieve—and was garnished with coriander leaves. The potatoes, sliced into two or four pieces, sat with meat chunks. It had a distinct wood fire smell because it was usually cooked for a long time in a pan on wood fire chulha. Every servant got a taamchini (enamel) bowl of curry with meat and potato pieces along with large rotis prepared on chulhas on an ulta tawa (inverted skillet). A serving bowl of the curry was sent to the table first. It was a quotidian dish, but we didn't have it every day as the Nawabs.

I love the aloo gosht cooked at my in-laws' place. It still tastes the same today minus the wood smell. We have regrettably converted to gas stove and the dish is now cooked in a pressure cooker. I miss the wood smell and the comfort of eating near the chulha in winters.

My husband often remarked that we can never replicate the aloo gosht he had at the royal tables. I asked several khansamas and ladies and tried out with finer points to no avail. Then one day, Akhtar Bhai, my cook, reproduced what Qamar said was the exact taste of the aloo gosht of yore. I asked Akhtar Bhai what he did differently.

'I cooked it the way we used to for the servants—dumped the meat, the masalas, topped it with oil and let it cook itself.'

So that was the key! All the elaborate sub-steps of braising the meat, frying onions, using garam masalas had obscured the simple, from the heart, wholesome meat curry. Rampur aloo gosht has just the basic masalas and no garam masalas or aromatics, unlike the Awadhi or Mughlai version. The Delhi version doesn't use turmeric and hence has a darker curry. The curry is thicker and darker in Lucknow and Delhi possibly due to the use of fried onions and garam masalas. Some people use tomatoes in the curry which makes it thicker, and the taste is completely different. Rampuris would shudder at the prospect of tomatoes in their curries unless it is tamatar gosht (tomato meat curry). The potatoes in the Awadhi curries are first shallow fried before they are added to the meat curry, altering its taste. An elaborate version of aloo gosht is served at wedding banquets at Lucknow. The humble potatoes look like they have wandered into the wrong curry!

The dish we can have every day of our lives is bhuna qeema (mincemeat sauté)—a quotidian dish of extraordinary flavour. Nawab Sayed Murtaza Ali Khan had a simple request when he came to my in-laws' house for dinner—'Ask Bhinno to cook qeema for me.' Bhinno was my mother-in-law's nickname. A brazier was set up for her in the lower veranda where she would sit on a stool and make the magical mincemeat.

By the time I came into the family, 'Bhinno' was bedridden; her cousin, Parveen Apa, taught me to cook the family speciality. Married into the qeema-loving family, I felt I had to master the dish. The dish was so simple that I was shocked at the hoo-ha around it. The secret was the coarsely chopped fresh, lean mincemeat. Parveen Apa never washed the mincemeat. She just fried half an onion, put it in the meat with ginger–garlic pastes, turmeric, coriander and chilli powders—and that was it! No water was ever added. It was sautéed in a lot of mustard oil and cooked in its own juices. No wonder they said you needed strong arms to 'bhuno' (sauté) it! Notwithstanding, I always end up instinctively crimping on the oil in keeping with my weight-watching sensibilities.

Aloo Gosht[3]

Aloo gosht is my favourite home-coming dish. Driving home on the highway, I call up Akhtar Bhai for an aloo gosht and dal-chawal meal—light and welcoming as a mother's love.

---

[3] The same method can be used for arvi gosht, substituting arvi (colocasia) for potatoes.

Ingredients

1/2 kg mutton
5 medium-sized potatoes, peeled and cut in half or 4 pieces
lengthwise
1/2 or 3/4 cup mustard oil
1 tbsp curd (optional)
3 medium-sized onions, roughly diced
1 tbsp garlic paste
1 tbsp ginger paste
1–2 tsp red chilli powder (or as per taste)
2 tsp coriander powder
1 tsp turmeric powder
Salt to taste

Method 1 (simple)

1. In a pressure cooker, add the meat, all the masalas and
   the onions. Pour the oil on top.[4] (Basically, add everything
   except potatoes.)
2. Depending on the toughness of meat, add 1 cup of water
   if using a pressure cooker or 2–3 cups if it is a pan, and
   cook over medium heat till the meat is done.
3. Sauté the meat on high flame adding splashes of water till
   the oil separates from the masalas.
4. Add the potatoes and pour 1/2 cup of water if cooking in
   a pressure cooker or 1 cup if cooking in a pan.

---

[4] You don't even need to smoke the mustard oil!

5. Keep cooking till the potatoes are done. They should not be overdone, or the curry will be spoilt. They should be firm and not crumbly. If they disintegrate into the curry, it will become mushy.

6. The curry should be on the thinner side, so if required, add boiled water to achieve the right consistency.

7. Garnish the dish with coriander leaves and serve.

Method 2 (elaborate)

1. Heat the oil in a pressure cooker till it starts to smoke. Lower the heat and add half of the onions. Fry till they turn golden. Some spices can be added too: 3-4 peppercorns, green cardamoms and cloves.

2. Add the meat and fry it. Add ginger and garlic pastes, curd and the rest of the onions.

3. Add red chilli, coriander and turmeric powders.

4. Sauté the meat on high flame, adding splashes of water till the oil separates from the masalas.

5. Depending on the toughness of the meat, add 1 cup of water if using a pressure cooker or 2-3 cups if using a pan, and cook over medium heat till the meat is done.

6. Add the potatoes and pour 1/2 cup of water if using a pressure cooker or 1 cup if using a pan.

7. Cook them till the potatoes are done. They should not be overdone, or the curry will be spoilt. They should be firm and not crumbly. If they disintegrate into the curry, it will become mushy.

8. The curry should be thin, so if required, add boiled water to achieve the right consistency.

9. Garnish the dish with coriander leaves and serve.

Hari Mirch Qeema

This is a favourite family recipe that my aunt-in-law,
Parveen Apa taught me. We don't use garam masalas.
It's an everyday dish.

Ingredients

1/2 kg lean meat, coarsely minced by hand
3/4–1 cup mustard oil (You can use less)
1 tbsp curd (optional)
2 medium onions, diced
1 tbsp garlic paste
1 tbsp ginger paste
1–2 tsp red chilli powder (or as per taste)
1 tsp coriander powder (optional)
1 tsp turmeric powder
5–6 large green chillies
1/2 tsp dried fenugreek leaves (kasoori methi) (optional)[5]
Salt to taste

Method

1. Heat the oil in a pressure cooker or a pan. Add half of the
   diced onions and fry them till they become golden.

---

[5] Some people prefer the fenugreek taste. I don't use it because I feel it
overpowers the taste of the green chillies.

2. Add the mincemeat and fry them for a bit. Then put in the rest of the spices and ginger–garlic pastes and keep frying. Add the chopped onions and salt. If the mincemeat is fresh, it can be fried without using water and it will become tender, otherwise use 1/2 cup of water and put on pressure for about 15 minutes.

3. Check if the meat is done. Add curd, green chillies and sauté till the excess water evaporates and the qeema is dry and the oil is visible. Tip: split and deseed the chillies if one is intolerant to spicy food.

4. Garnish the dish with chopped coriander and serve.

Qeema Shimla Mirch / Matar Qeema / Qeema Aloo / Karonda Qeema

The basic qeema sauté is a versatile dish open to seasonal vegetables. People even cook qeema in a curry form when there is less mince available.

Ingredients

1/2 kg minced lean meat
3/4 to 1 cup mustard oil
1 tbsp curd
1 medium-sized onion, diced
1 tbsp garlic paste
1 tbsp ginger paste

1 tsp red chilli powder (or as per taste)
1 tsp coriander powder
1 tsp turmeric powder
250 gm green peas / 3 large capsicums, chopped thin lengthwise
or in small squares / 2–3 large potatoes, cut in four pieces
lengthwise / 100 gm karonda, deseeded and cut in two
4–5 green chillies
Salt to taste

Method

1. Heat oil in a pressure cooker or a pan. Add the diced
   onions and fry them till they become golden.
2. Add the mincemeat and fry them for a bit. Add the rest of
   the spices, ginger–garlic pastes and curd and keep frying
   till the garlic smell disappears. Add the salt.
3. If the mincemeat is fresh, it can be fried without using
   water, and it will become tender; otherwise, use 1/2 cup
   of water and pressure cook it for about 15 minutes.
4. Check if the meat is done. Add the green chillies and
   green peas/potatoes/capsicums/karonda and pressure
   cook on medium heat till the vegetables are done. Add a
   little water, if needed.
5. Sauté till the excess water evaporates and the qeema is dry
   and the oil is visible.
6. Garnish the dish with chopped coriander and serve.

Palak Qeema

Mincemeat with spinach. This is cooked rarely at my place because my husband and son have a look that says—'what are these leaves doing in my qeema?'

Ingredients

1/2 kg minced lean meat
1/2 kg chopped spinach
3/4 cup mustard oil
1 tbsp curd
1 medium-sized onion, diced
1 tbsp garlic paste
1 tbsp ginger paste
1 tsp red chilli powder (or as per taste)
1 tsp coriander powder
1 tsp turmeric powder
4–5 green chillies
1 tsp dried fenugreek leaves (kasoori methi) or 1 tbsp fresh leaves, chopped (optional)
Salt to taste

Method

1. Heat the oil in a pressure cooker or a pan. Add the diced onions and fry them till they become golden.
2. Add the mincemeat and fry them for a bit. Add the rest of the spices, ginger–garlic pastes, curd and chopped spinach. Put on pressure or cook till the mincemeat is done.

3. Add green chillies and fenugreek leaves. There might be excess water so cook on high heat till the water evaporates.
4. Start sautéing till the mincemeat is dry and the oil is visible.
5. Garnish the dish with chopped coriander and serve.

Karela Qeema

I love the slight bitter tang with the mincemeat. Generally, Rampuris mount a war against the bitterness of the gourd— they wash it, sun it and boil it till it loses even its essential bitterness.

Ingredients

1/2 kg minced lean meat
1/2 kg small karela or bitter gourd
1 cup mustard oil
6–7 medium-sized onions, diced
2 tbsp slightly sour curd
1 tbsp garlic paste
1 tbsp ginger paste
1 tsp red chilli powder (or as per taste)
1 tsp coriander powder
1 tsp turmeric powder
Salt to taste

Method

1. Scrape the bitter gourds and remove the seeds. Reserve the seeds. Rub salt on the bitter gourds and set them aside for 2 hours. Wash out the salt well in running water and cut the gourds into 1 inch thick rings. If you don't like the slightly bitter tang of the gourds, boil them for 5 minutes and drain the water to remove the bitterness.

2. Heat the oil in a pressure cooker or a pan till it starts to smoke. Reduce the flame. Fry the bitter gourd pieces and the seeds till they become golden. Drain them and remove them from oil.

3. Fry half of the onions till they turn golden. Add the mincemeat and fry them for a bit. Add the rest of the spices and ginger–garlic pastes. Pour 1/2 cup of water and pressure cook till the meat is done.

4. Add the gourd pieces, curds and sauté till the excess water evaporates. If the bitter gourd is already boiled, then add them after the water is evaporated. Check that the bitter gourd and mincemeat are tender.

5. Sauté till the mincemeat is dry and the oil is visible.

6. Serve it hot with roti or parathas.

Qeema Bharey Kareley

Bitter gourd with mincemeat stuffing.
No one in my family appreciates this combination and it is so time consuming that I almost never cook it, but I just love

the dish and ask Mamma to get it prepared for me when I
visit her.

Ingredients

1/2 kg finely minced lean meat
1/2 kg medium-sized karela or bitter gourd
1 cup mustard oil
4–5 medium-sized onions, diced
1 tbsp garlic paste
1 tbsp ginger paste
1 tsp red chilli powder (or as per taste)
1 tsp coriander powder
1 tsp turmeric powder
Salt to taste

Method

1. Scrape the bitter gourds and remove the seeds. Rub salt
   on the bitter gourds and set them aside for 2 hours.
   Wash out the salt well in running water. Boil the bitter
   gourd for 5 minutes, and drain the water to remove the
   bitterness.
2. Heat the oil in a pressure cooker or a pan till it starts to
   smoke. Reduce the flame. Lightly fry the bitter gourd till
   they change colour. Drain and remove them from oil. Set
   on kitchen tissue to remove excess oil.
3. Fry half of the onions till they turn golden. Add the
   mincemeat and fry them for a bit. Add the rest of the
   spices and ginger–garlic pastes. Pour 1/2 cup of water and
   pressure cook till the meat is done.

4. Cook on high flame and let all the water evaporate from the mincemeat; then sauté it till it is completely dry.
5. Stuff the bitter gourds with mincemeat and tie them with thread.
6. In a frying pan, heat oil. Place the stuffed gourds on it and fry them. Turn them so that all sides are fried and golden. Reduce the heat and cover the pan. Let them cook till the skin becomes soft and well done.

Qeema Stew / Mincemeat Stew

The stew is the laziest dish to cook when you want something good to eat without much effort. If you leave out the garam masalas, you can use it in pasta, as a pie base or simply in sandwiches.

Ingredients

1/2 kg minced lean meat
1/2 kg onions, diced
1 cup mustard oil
6–7 cloves
3 black cardamoms
3–4 bay leaves
10 peppercorns
1/2 inch piece cinnamon
1 garlic head, finely chopped

1 inch ginger, finely chopped
3-4 dried red chillies (or as per taste)
1 cup curd
Salt to taste

Method

1. Heat the oil till it smokes. Add half of the onions and fry them till they turn translucent. Add the cloves, cardamoms, cinnamon, bay leaves and peppercorns.
2. Add the mincemeat and fry them.
3. Add the rest of the ingredients and pressure cook till the mincemeat is done. If needed, use 1/2 cup of water. Some people prefer to use ginger paste rather than ginger juliennes.
4. Cook it on high flame and let the excess water evaporate; then sauté till the mincemeat is dry and the oil is visible.
5. Serve hot with roti or paratha.

Bhindi Gosht[6]

Meat and okra curry.
This is one dish my daughter Gaeti cooks well. Most of the time she aspires not to cook. She is genetically disposed to being an occasional cook and a foodie.

---

[6] This same recipe can work using peas or lobia beans with meat.

Ingredients

1/2 kg lean meat
250 gm small-sized bhindi or okra
3/4 cup mustard oil
1 medium-sized onion, chopped
1 tbsp garlic paste
1 tbsp ginger paste
1 tbsp onion paste
2 tsp coriander powder
1 tsp turmeric powder
1 tsp red chilli powder
Salt to taste

Method

1. Heat oil till it smokes. Add the chopped onions and fry them till they become golden.
2. Add and fry the meat. Lower the flame.
3. Mix ginger, garlic and onion pastes with the rest of the spices in a bowl (you may add a little water to make a paste), and add this mixture to the meat.
4. Sauté the meat, adding splashes of water to avoid the masala from getting burnt. Keep sautéing till the oil separates.
5. Add 1 cup of water and pressure cook till the meat is done.
6. Wash the okra, chop off the top and lower ends and cut them into 2 inch pieces. In a frying pan, add 4 teaspoons of oil and lightly fry the okra pieces on low heat, turning them till they become slightly brown in places.

7. Add the fried okra to the meat. If required, add 1/2 cup of water and put on simmer till the vegetable becomes tender.
8. Let the excess water evaporate. The texture should be thick.

Palak Gosht

Meat and spinach curry.
This is again looked at in askance by my husband and son but better tolerated than palak qeema. I prefer using homegrown spinach for this. Store-bought spinach is slightly mature and probably has oodles of pesticide, which spoils the taste. One can grow spinach quite easily in planters. It is a matter of devotion.

Ingredients

1/2 kg lean meat
1/2 kg chopped spinach
3/4 cup mustard oil
1 medium-sized onion, finely chopped
1 tbsp garlic paste
1 tbsp ginger paste
1 tbsp onion paste
1 tsp coriander powder

1 tsp turmeric powder
1 tsp red chilli powder
1 tsp dried fenugreek leaves (kasoori methi) (optional)
Salt to taste

For the garnish

1 bunch of coriander leaves, chopped

Method

1. Heat the oil till it smokes. Add the chopped onions and fry them till they become golden.
2. Put in the meat and fry it. Lower the flame.
3. Mix ginger, garlic and onion pastes with the rest of the spices in a bowl (you may add a little water to make a paste) and add this mixture to the meat.
4. Sauté the meat, adding splashes of water to avoid the masala from getting burnt. Keep sautéing till the oil separates.
5. Add spinach and half a cup of water and pressure cook till the meat is done.
6. Add fenugreek leaves and let the excess water evaporate. The texture should be thick.
7. Garnish the dish with chopped coriander leaves and serve.

Chuqandar Gosht

Meat and beetroot curry.
This colourful dish is a favoured item on our table. The
sweetness of the beetroot must be balanced with the tartness
of tomatoes. The hybrid tomatoes barely have any tartness,
so we need to add more of them.

Ingredients

1/2 kg lean meat
400 gm beetroots (without leaves), grated
3/4 cup mustard oil
1 medium-sized onion, finely chopped
3–4 medium-sized tomatoes, chopped
1 tbsp garlic paste
1 tbsp ginger paste
1 tbsp onion paste
1 tsp coriander powder
1 tsp turmeric powder
1 tsp red chilli powder
Salt to taste

For the garnish

5–6 green chillies, slit lengthwise (seeds may be removed)
1 bunch of coriander leaves, chopped

Method

1. Heat the oil till it smokes. Add the chopped onions and fry them till they become golden.
2. Add the meat and fry it. Lower the flame.
3. Mix ginger, garlic and onion pastes with the rest of the spices in a bowl (you may add a little water to make a paste) and add them to the meat.
4. Sauté the meat, adding splashes of water to avoid the masala from getting burnt. Keep sautéing till the oil separates.
5. Add the beetroots and tomatoes. Add 1 cup of water and pressure cook till the meat is done and the beetroots become soft.
6. Let the excess water evaporate. Sauté to make the beetroots thick and mushy.
7. Garnish the dish with chopped coriander leaves and green chillies and serve.

Shalgam Gosht

Meat and turnip curry.
Rampur has local turnips with very small bulbs and thick foliage. It tastes completely different from the usual big bulbed turnips available everywhere.

Ingredients

1/2 kg lean meat
400 gm turnips with leaves
200 gm or 1 bunch of spinach, finely chopped
3/4 cup mustard oil
1 medium-sized onion, finely chopped
1 tbsp garlic paste
1 tbsp ginger paste
1 tbsp onion paste
1 tsp coriander powder
1 tsp turmeric powder
1 tsp red chilli powder
Salt to taste

For the garnish

5-6 green chillies, slit lengthwise (seeds may be removed)
1 bunch of coriander leaves, chopped

Method

1. Chop the turnip leaves (discard the stems) and cut the turnip bulbs into small pieces.
2. Heat oil till it smokes. Add the chopped onions and fry them till they become golden.
3. Add the meat and fry it. Lower the flame.
4. Mix ginger, garlic and onion pastes with the rest of the spices in a bowl and add to the meat.

5. Sauté the meat, adding splashes of water to avoid the masala from getting burnt. Keep sautéing till the oil separates.

6. Add the chopped vegetables. Add 1 cup of water and pressure cook till the meat is done and the turnips become soft.

7. Let the excess water evaporate. Sauté to make the curry thick and mushy.

8. Garnish the dish with chopped coriander leaves and green chillies and serve.

Rampuri Stew

'Ishtoo', as the khansamas call it, was possibly a hybrid creation of Indian and British cuisines. We added a lot of garam masalas to it and sautéed it—in the true Indian style—till the onions became mushy and the oil became visible.

Ingredients

1/2 kg meat, lean or with bones
1/2 kg onions, diced
1 cup mustard oil
1 garlic head, finely chopped
1 inch ginger, finely chopped
6-7 cloves

2 black cardamoms, crushed
3–4 bay leaves
10 peppercorns
1/2 inch piece cinnamon
I tsp cumin
1 mace
1/4 nutmeg, crushed
3–4 dried red chillies (or as per taste)
1 cup curd
Salt to taste

Method

1. In a pressure cooker, heat the oil till it smokes. Add half of the onions and fry them till they turn translucent.
2. Add all the garam masalas. Put the meat into the masalas and fry. Add the rest of the onions, ginger, garlic, curd, salt, chillies and 1 cup of water. Pressure cook till the meat and the onions are tender. If cooking in a pan, use 2 cups of water.
3. Let the excess water evaporate and sauté till oil is visible.
4. Serve it hot.

Twelve

Angrezi Khana and the Khansama

There was nothing Chinese about the 'cheeni sabzi' that Bhura khansama served with flourish at the special dinner for Nawab Sayed Murtaza Ali Khan (1923–82) at our Aligarh home in 1972. The dish was a medley of finely chopped vegetables—which possibly prompted the moniker—swimming in a meat stock gravy. My grandfather had hosted the dinner to celebrate his son's wedding, and Bhura khansama had been specially called from Rampur to cook this dinner. Bhura Bhai awed the guests with his vast repertoire of the angrezi khana that he had learnt to cook at the Khasbagh Palace kitchens. There were roasts, mutton chaap, fish puffs and puddings vying for a place on the table with the usual Rampur menu—yakhni pulao, qorma and gulathhi. Bhura Bhai was asked to teach the new daughter-in-law English cuisine—a comparatively bland fare diligently served to my grandfather for lunch because it was considered healthier than the rich Rampur cuisine. My grandmother turned up her nose at the, what she called, basainda (smelly) food her poor husband was subjected to.

British and continental dishes found their way into the Rampur cuisine in the twentieth century when the Nawabs started entertaining British officials and diplomats. A separate angrezi kitchen became part of the royal kitchens as early as 1889 during the time of Nawab Sayed Hamid Ali Khan— as per the Administrative Report of 1889-90—or maybe even earlier. Subsequently, the Nawabs sent their khansamas to Paris and London for training. Irshad Khan khansama, was sent by Nawab Sayed Raza Ali Khan to Paris to learn the art of baking. He established the 'Rainbow Bakeries' in 1954, and it is still renowned for its Danish cookies, shortcakes and biscuits. Nawab Hamid's successor, Nawab Sayed Raza Ali Khan was an anglophile, and it was during his reign that English cuisine became a part of the daily fare. Princess Mehrunnisa Begum, daughter of Nawab Sayed Raza Ali Khan, writes in her memoir, An Extraordinary Life, that they had a choice of both Indian and English cuisines, and 'all the best European foods' graced the tables. The young prince and princesses were brought up in the royal nursery under the care of British nannies. They were served a typical English breakfast of Quaker oats, juice, eggs, fresh fish from the Arabian Sea, jams from England, cheese from Switzerland and wholewheat bread. Nawab Sayed Raza Ali Khan was fond of western cuisine and often had porridge for breakfast and a roast and salad meal at noon.

What emerged from these fusions and improvisations was a new anglicized, haute cuisine, emulated by the elite classes through their khansamas. The cooks from British settlements

in neighbouring Moradabad and Bareilly possibly contributed
to this 'anglicization' of the cuisine. We know from written
and oral accounts that the Nawabs and other aristocratic
families enjoyed their soups, cutlets and roasts. Nawab Sayed
Raza Ali Khan used to have a light English luncheon as did
some other members of the royal family. Dinners, which
consisted of Indian dishes, were more elaborate. Nawab
Sayed Raza Ali Khan, a diabetic, had a severely restricted diet
unlike his predecessor, Nawab Sayed Hamid Ali Khan. The
latter ate only once a day after seven in the evening. Princess
Mehrunnisa writes that his dinner—an elaborate Rampuri
meal, meat-heavy and spicy—was a 'dietician's nightmare'. An
inadvertent follower of the OMAD (One Meal a Day) diet,
the gentleman remained slim and spry till the end.

There was an inclination towards emulating British
lifestyle among the royals and elites in the time of Nawab
Raza. The easily adapted elements of culture like food
and dress were seamlessly assimilated into the aristocratic
lifestyle. The young prince and princesses in their suits,
frocks and bonnets were sent to British-run schools and
boarding establishments in Mussoorie in the 1930s—a
trend mirrored by other elite families of Rampur. My
mother and her siblings were educated at La Martinere
School, Lucknow, in the 1940s and 1950s. Just like other
males associated with the Rampur court, my grandfather
had a typical British wardrobe of day suits, dinner jackets
and summer suits, which were maintained by his personal
servant. Every winter, for years after he passed away, we
took out and sunned the gentleman's wardrobe and stories.
My Nami Amma, like most Rampuri women, continued

to wear her ghararas and follow the rhythms of the conservative Rampur life. The khansamas were taught the angrezi khana, which soon became 'sahib ka khana'. The ladies often found it too bland for their tastes, but their boarding-school educated children enjoyed the English and Continental cuisines. Ameer Ahmad Khan, my grandfather-in-law and Nawab Sayed Raza Ali Khan's chief secretary, got his personal servant trained in angrezi khana by the Nawab's cook. A similar arrangement took place at my grandfather's household where Attu khansama (of the stiff sewain fame), trained by Nawab's cook, attempted the angrezi dishes. The daughters tried their hands at recipes gleaned from *Women's Weekly, Women's Realm*—British magazines that were eagerly awaited every month. My aunts recall Babban khansama presenting his signature dish, ass-no-cream, to be met with riotous laughter. Offended, Babban attempted to explain the name of the sweetmeat—'ass' means baraf, 'no' means nahi and 'cream' is cream. Probably what he meant was 'as snow cream'! Thus, the English cuisine was carried from the royal kitchens to the elite kitchens and most of the aristocratic families wanted to embrace the occasional English and continental meal, setting a high premium on the khansamas who were trained in its preparation.

Mehrunnisa Begum writes that the per-year kitchen expenses of Nawab Sayed Hamid Ali Khan were 250,000 rupees on Indian kitchens and 1,50,000 rupees on English kitchens. In current terms, it would approximately translate to an annual expenditure of 8.3 crores on Indian kitchens and 4.5 crores on English kitchens. The modern Khasbagh palace built by Nawab Sayed Hamid Ali Khan had a kitchen block behind the palace with coal bhattis for cooking.[1] It was divided into an Indian kitchen, a dessert kitchen, an English kitchen and stores supervised by the munsarim (administrator). The menu for the day was communicated by the Nawab or his Begum to the munsarim.

Generally, the elite Rampur households consisted of at least one khansama assisted by junior cooks. Sir Abdus Samad Khan, the prime minister of Nawab Sayed Hamid Ali Khan, had three khansamas who presided over three kitchens— the Indian, English and dessert kitchens. The khansamas, assisted by a small team of sous chefs, reigned supreme over their kitchens. The kitchen block was situated between the mardana and zenana sections allowing access from both sides. The khansamas and the kitchen staff were all males. The lady of the house decided the menu or a part of the menu because there were some regular dishes that had to be there in large quantities for the servants. English cuisine or Indianized versions of English dishes were served daily. Thus, Irish stew was tempered with fried onions, Indian spices were added to the chops, stews and roasts to suit the Rampuri palate; the English custards and puddings were made sweeter. Even today if the sweetmeat has less sugar, the cook or lady of the house is told that it tastes like angrezi meetha.

Majid khansama is the last in the line of royal khansamas. Always dressed in a white kurta-pyjama, navy blue bandgala coat and Hamid cap, he is the doyen of the Rampur khansama tradition. Majid khansama's father, Ashiq khansama, was the

---

[1] Majid khansama who worked there from the 1960s described the kitchens as having coal-fired bhatti (ovens) in a long row at the centre.

head cook of the Nawab's angrezi kitchen. Nawab Sayed Raza Ali Khan had sent him abroad to learn English and French cuisine. After the Nawab's death in 1966, Ashiq khansama continued to work for Nawab Sayed Murtaza Ali Khan. The privy purse given to the Nawabs after the merger of Rampur into the Indian Union was barely enough to maintain the vast palaces and kitchens. There was considerable downsizing in the royal lifestyle and several khansamas were asked to leave; some moved down the social ladder—from serving aristocratic to middle-class households—to find employment, while others set up small shops to sell kababs, pulaos and sweets. When he was about sixteen years of age, Majid was called by Nawab Murtaza and was asked to join the royal kitchens to learn from his father Ashiq khansama. This was the usual method of apprenticeship in the Nawab's kitchens. Majid learnt to cook English dishes from his father and his uncle and worked at the royal kitchens.

Majid khansama became a part of my household when I got married in 1990. We rarely ate at home in those early years, preferring to go to my in-laws' place for most of our meals. It must have been quite a comedown for the khansama. I can imagine his frustration for he got few occasions to flaunt his talents. Majid Bhai tried to teach me the English dishes, which were his speciality, but food was the last thing on my mind at that time. Though I enjoyed the roasts and cutlets he prepared, I preferred the delectable fare to appear magically at the dining table. I loved the way he served the food holding the tray shoulder high. Our house is a colonial bungalow, and the kitchen was situated in a separate block at that time. The food was great, but the kitchen was a mess. My husband defended Majid Bhai—a khansama was not supposed to wash dishes or clean up—who didn't have any sous-chefs or even a maidservant to clean up after him.

When we moved away from Rampur, Majid Bhai returned to the royal ambit and presided over the kitchens of Nawab Sayed Murtaza Ali Khan's daughter, Princess Naghat Abedi, for nearly three decades till 2020, when he sought voluntary retirement. We watched him assisting the princess in the food shows on YouTube videos, which burst forth on our screens after 2010. He is there in the coffee table books on royal cuisines, mixing the masalas and skewering the meats. The princess guarded him like a precious jewel, and he had young sous chefs to train and boss around. A confirmed bachelor, Majid Bhai used the earnings from the job to marry off his sisters and help his family in Rampur. Though he was only 200 kilometres from Rampur, he was constantly homesick like all khansamas. He finally took retirement from his job, handing over the mantle to two non-Rampuri sous chefs who, he feels, are undeserving of his precious knowledge. I believe, like all khansamas, he too withheld the finer points of his culinary knowledge. Though he is well provided for by the princess, he craves the glamour and excitement of grand royal dinners. The princess, herself a culinary afficionado, keeps a resplendent table of Rampuri cuisine at her Delhi home. Majid Bhai comes over sometimes to cook for us and attempts to teach me again. With my recent interest in Rampur cuisine, he finds me an attentive pupil.

Rampuri Crumb Chops

The 'Cram Chaap', as Majid Bhai calls them, requires very specific kind of mutton ribs. Twice we had to abandon the cooking plan because the chops were not cut properly.

Ingredients

1 kg mutton chops (the chops must have a sizeable amount of meat on them. 4–5 ribs should make one chop.)
250 gm ghee or refined oil
2 medium-sized onions, chopped finely (optional)
4–5 green chillies, chopped finely (optional)
1–2 tsp red chilli powder (or as per taste)
1/2 cup refined flour
2 eggs
1/2 cup breadcrumbs

For the marinade

2 tsp mustard powder
2 tbsp Worcestershire sauce
1 tbsp red vinegar
Salt to taste

Method

1. Thoroughly wash the chops and dry them on a kitchen towel. Flatten the meat portion by beating it with a knife. Dip them in the prepared marinade and set aside for 1–2 hours.

2. Beat the eggs and add the onions and green chillies.
3. On a plate, mix the refined flour and breadcrumbs.
4. Heat the oil in a frying pan. Dip the chops in the egg mixture, roll them on the breadcrumbs. If the breadcrumbs are made in a mixer–grinder, sift it through a flour sieve.
5. Shallow fry the chops till golden.
6. Serve them hot with tomato sauce.

Mincemeat Cutlets

A favourite breakfast dish of the Anglophile Rampuri;
referred to as 'cutluss' by the khansamas.

Ingredients

1 kg lean meat, minced fine
Ghee or refined oil for shallow frying
3 eggs
5–8 green chillies, chopped finely
2 medium-sized onions, finely chopped
1 bunch of coriander leaves, finely chopped
1–2 tsp red chilli powder (optional)
1/2 cup refined flour1/2 cup breadcrumbs
2 tsp mustard powder
2 tbsp Worcestershire sauce
1 tsp garam masala powder

2 tsp ground black pepper
1 bread loaf

Method

1. Heat 1 tablespoon of oil and fry half of the onions in it till translucent. Add the mincemeat and sauté till its moisture evaporates. Add red chilli powder, salt and 1 cup of water. Let it simmer till it is tender. Let the excess water evaporate. It should be absolutely dry. Set it aside to cool. (Some cooks add 3–4 cloves and 1–2 green cardamoms to take away the mincemeat smell.)

2. Add mustard powder and Worcestershire sauce to the mincemeat and mix well. Add 1 egg. Break the bread loaf into small pieces and mix them into it. Add the green chillies, chopped coriander and the rest of the onions. Check the salt.

3. Take tiny portions of the mixture and shape them into flat, tear-shaped patties and set them aside.

4. Beat the eggs. On a plate, mix the refined flour and breadcrumbs. If the breadcrumbs are made in a mixer-grinder, sift that through a flour sieve.

5. Heat the oil in a deep pan.

6. Dip the patties in the egg mixture, roll them on the breadcrumbs and deep fry them till they turn reddish brown.

7. Serve them hot with tomato sauce.

Potato Cutlets

Sometimes steamed mixed vegetables are mashed with potatoes. Some people even add mincemeat to mashed potatoes.

Ingredients

750 gm potatoes (preferably pahadi aloo)[2]
1/2 litre ghee or refined oil
3 eggs
2 medium-sized onions, finely chopped
4–5 green chillies, finely chopped
1 bunch of coriander leaves, chopped finely
1–2 tsp red chilli powder (or as per taste)
1 cup breadcrumbs
2 tsp mustard powder
2 tbsp Worcestershire sauce
1 tsp garam masala powder.
2 tsp ground black pepper
1 bread loaf

Method

1. Boil, peel and mash the potatoes.
2. Add mustard powder, Worcestershire sauce, red chilli powder and salt. Mix them well.
3. Beat 1 egg and add it to the potato mash.

---

[2] Pahadi aloo is generally grown in the mineral-rich soil of Uttarakhand and tastes much better than the ordinary potato.

4. Add the green chillies, chopped coriander and the onions.[3] Check the salt.
5. Shape tiny portions of the mixture into flat, tear-shaped patties and set them aside.
6. Beat 2 eggs. Spread the breadcrumbs on a plate. If the breadcrumbs are made in a mixer–grinder, sift that through a flour sieve.
7. Heat the oil in a deep pan.
8. Dip the patties in the egg mixture, then roll them in the breadcrumbs and deep fry them till they turn reddish brown.
9. Serve them hot with tomato sauce.

Fried Fish Fillet

An old Rampuri cookbook, *Shahi Dastarkhwan*, which used to be given to new brides of the family had this recipe. It surprisingly called for an anchovy sauce.

Ingredients

1/2 kg fish fillet, preferably Rohu
3/4 cup oil
1 tsp red chilli powder
1 onion, diced into tiny square pieces

---

[3] Half cup of peas can be used. Boil and mash them well and mix it into the potato mix. Adjust the seasoning accordingly.

1/2 cup refined flour
6 tsp anchovy sauce or fish sauce
2 eggs
2 green chillies, thinly sliced
1 tsp salt (or as per taste)

Method

1. The fish should be cut parallel to the spine and the inside cleaned. Remove the head and the tail. If this process of gutting the fish seems hard to manage, the fish fillets available in the market can be used instead.
2. Make a batter of all the ingredients, except oil.
3. Marinate the fish or dip the fillets in the batter and fry them till golden.

Mish-mash

Mish-mash with toast is another favourite breakfast fare. It's very like our anda bhujia.

Ingredients

4 eggs
1 tbsp ghee or oil
1 onion, finely diced
1 tomato, finely diced

2–3 green chillies, finely sliced
2 green or red peppers, julienned
1 tsp fresh ground black pepper
2 tbsp coriander leaves, chopped finely
100 gm cheese, grated
Salt to taste

Method

1. In an omelette pan, heat the ghee and add the onions. Fry them till they turn golden.
2. Add the tomatoes and let them cook on simmer.
3. Add green chillies and green peppers and continue to cook.
4. Beat the eggs and pour it in the pan. Sauté it on low heat.
5. Add cheese, salt and pepper. Add herbs, like oregano, for added flavour.
6. Sauté the mix till the eggs are done yet remain soft.

Thirteen

The Intricacies of Forgotten Sweetness

'When you put a piece of halwa sohan or habshi halwa in your mouth, it starts melting immediately. The taste is heavenly, and it never sticks to the tooth or irritates the throat. If you eat the halwa sohan cooked by a Rampur khansama, you would forget Abdurrazaq khansama's halwa served at Ghanta Ghar,[1] Delhi.'

Ahwal e Riyasat e Rampur
—Sayed Asghar Ali Shadani

The test of the famed Rampuri halwa sohan[2] or habshi halwa of yore was that when the halwa was put on a dish, one couldn't see any ghee on it. But when a finger was placed on the halwa, the ghee would gather around the finger; once the

---

[1] This is a reference to Ghanteywaley Halwai in Chandni Chowk; one of the oldest shops, it was established in 1790. It closed down in 2015 due to falling sales.

[2] Very often, people call it sohan halwa, but in Rampur, we refer to it as halwa sohan, a practice coming from the Urdu way of referring to halwas.

finger was removed, the ghee would get absorbed back into the halwa. This is remarkable considering that the quantity of ghee used was ten to twelve times that of the flour. The preparation of halwa sohan is a long-drawn-out process as the base of the halwa is samnak or wheat germ flour. The wheat grains take at least three to four days to germinate, and great care has to be taken while germinating the wheat. The grains must be sifted carefully to ensure that no broken or blackened grains are soaked or else the wheat germ will blacken and change the colour and the taste of the halwa. The blemished seeds might also decay and cause foul smell that can spoil the samnak. The perfect seeds are separated and wrapped in a cloth, which is kept moist but never wet. When the sprouts are about an inch long, they are dried and then ground to obtain the samnak flour. Oral history, narrated by Rampur cooks, credits the royal hakims for creating the recipe for halwa sohan and other halwas. As halwa sohan is popular in Afghanistan and in parts of Pakistan too, we can assume that the Rohillas carried the rustic samnak halwa to India where it was made more elaborate in the royal kitchens. Muneeza Shamsie declares she has never had the halwa sohan she used to have at Khasbagh Palace in the 1960s.

The origin of the sweetmeat may be traced back to a toffee biscuit like Iranian sweet called the sohan, which is made of wheat samnak, flour, butter and eggs. In Rampur, halwa sohan is cooked through the night, especially before a wedding or a grand celebration. The cooks are given a corner of the courtyard where they set up an open, makeshift chulha. A large kadhai is set over wood fire, and the halwa preparation continues as the guests arrive with gifts and sing songs for the

bride-to-be. It used to be the preferred sweet for distribution—
to the groom's family and guests—after the nikah ceremony.
Square pieces of the halwa are packed in boxes bearing the
names of the newlyweds. The in-laws are given several boxes.
My brother's wife is from Lucknow, and her family fell in love
with the halwa when they first tasted it. They even preserved
some of it for more than a year. A well-cooked halwa sohan
doesn't go bad for a long time and requires no refrigeration.

Nasreen Begum, married to Nawab Sayed Raza Ali Khan's
nephew, remembers cooking the halwa sohan at home with
the help of her khansamas. The old khansamas have passed
away, and she is now too old to supervise the cooking, so she
must depend on the local halwai for her requirement. There
are hardly any khansamas willing to cook it at home these days
because it takes eight to nine hours to cook; people usually
order halwa sohan from the local shops for special occasions.

Halwa sohan is considered a winter sweet, and I remember,
we used to get boxes from Amanat Bhai's old shop every
winter. *Amanat Bhai ki lal dukaan* in the qila area is known
for the best halwa sohan in Rampur. Amanat Bhai Sr used to
prepare sweets for Nawab Sayed Raza Ali Khan and Nawab
Sayed Murtaza Ali Khan. There are now three 'Amanat
Bhai shops' from the different branches of the old maestro's
family, each claiming to have the genuine handwritten or oral
recipe. However, the taste and texture of the halwa sohan
has undergone a complete change over the years—even from
the time of my childhood. The texture was finer, each piece
coalesced into a cohesive satisfying whole, with barely visible
ghee and no jarring, greasy aftertaste. The halwa now has a
thick, grainy texture and is more crumbly. It definitely does

not taste the same. I believe that the ingredients and their proportions have altered due to higher costs incurred by the halwai and lesser paying ability of the customers. The use of ghee substitutes instead of genuine ghee contributes to the undesirable aftertaste. The colour is a much darker brown with speckles of frozen ghee—very different from the earlier reddish brown. These days, the favoured nikah sweets are boondi laddus and not the usual halwa sohan because most Rampuris, like me, feel that it doesn't taste the same anymore.

I visited Amanat Bhai's lal dukaan near the old post office right outside the qila to inquire about the reason for the devolution of the halwa sohan. Haris Raza, Amanat Bhai's grandson, tends to the shop now. The workshop is right above the tiny, unimpressive shop with faded awnings. At less than 500 rupees a kilo, the halwa sohan caters to the pocket of the ordinary man. Haris makes special halwa sohan for the members of the royal family using large quantities of pure ghee. But even the special halwa sohan has the same grainy texture and a burnt, dark brown look. The caramel taste is overpowering. Haris blames it on the changing taste of the customers. He nods when I describe the halwa sohan from my childhood, 'Khaane pe ghee ki pichkaari nikalti thi'—with every bite, there was a squirt of ghee in the mouth—he says.

He showed me the samnak flour and the wheat germ, which was in the process of germinating in his kitchen workshop. He had reduced the amount of ghee and sugar. The proportion of the ingredients used in halwa sohan is thirty litres of milk, a kilo of samnak flour, two kilos of semolina, two kilos of ghee and seven kilos of sugar. Comparing the current proportions of ingredients to those prescribed in the old cookbook texts

I was able to make the following observations. Semolina was never used in the old recipes. Maida or refined flour was used with samnak to form the base of the halwa. The use of semolina in double the proportion of samnak has resulted in the change in texture, colour and taste. Moreover, the proportion of ghee has been reduced drastically and the quantity of sugar has been increased probably to overpower other tastes or the lack thereof. Every halwai knows that it is the samnak flour that absorbs the ghee, and if we reduce samnak, we need to reduce ghee; on the other hand, if we decide to reduce ghee, we must reduce samnak or the halwa would appear too dry. Haris says he is following his father's recipe. So, at some point, the substitutions and change in proportions took place maybe due to lack of availability of samnak, or the tedious procedure of preparing the samnak flour, resulting in a completely different taste of halwa sohan.

The sweet caramel taste of the halwa and its reddish-brown colour were achieved after a long period of sautéing in the kadhai. It used to take six hours to cook. Now, halwa sohan is cooked for nine hours because people prefer a darker shade of brown. According to Haris, even the erstwhile royal family demands less ghee and over-sautéed halwa. Haris has started making the aloe vera halwa along the lines of halwa sohan because of its high demand in the winters to ease joint pains. As per the written and oral histories, aloe vera halwa was never cooked in Rampur and adrak halwa was the 'joint pain halwa fix'.

Haris enlightens me on the finer points of halwa-making as I watch the cooks intent on the large steaming kadhais, furiously sautéing the halwa. The halwai adds a little phitkari (alum) at the right time to curdle the milk and effect a 'daana' or grainy texture to the halwa. The curdling of the milk is an integral sub process which gives a unique texture to the halwa. Afghani cooks generally use curd to curdle the milk. Most halwais commit the mistake of adding the entire milk to the flour. The flour should be dissolved in just enough milk to make a thick paste. The rest of the milk should be added in splashes while sautéing. The intensity of sauté, the judgement of colour and the timing of adding the ingredients one after another comes after years of practice. The resultant caramelized taste of the halwa with its fine texture is to die for. Some prefer to warm it up to make it soft, but I like it chewy. This method of preparing halwa sohan is similar to the one followed in Multan and Afghanistan and probably has its culinary roots from there.

Haris Googles my profile and promises to make the old-style halwa for me. I took him up on his promise on my son's wedding in 2021. Though there was an overwhelming vote in support of boondi laddus, I wanted to distribute the old-style halwa sohan as nikah sweet. The family reluctantly agreed only if the halwa was good enough. Haris was kind enough to send us samples, take feedback and modify the halwa. After three rounds of sampling, the halwa was pronounced somewhat close to, though not quite, the halwa of our collective food memories. Four pieces of halwa were packed into shining boxes and handed out to the guests after the nikah. The halwa sohan afficionados requested for several boxes.

Doodhiya halwa sohan is a variant of halwa sohan and is quite popular in Rampur. Samnak and wheat flour form the base of this halwa. The flours are dissolved in milk and cooked. It has the same ingredients as the halwa sohan but the lesser proportion of milk and ghee changes the colour and the taste of doodhiya halwa.

Oral history, cited in writings on Rampur cuisine, speaks of the adrak halwa. It is said that one of the Nawabs, suffering from joint aches, was prescribed ginger or a ginger-based medicine. Since he detested ginger, the cooks were asked to cleverly devise a ginger-halwa for the Nawab so he would never suspect that he was being fed the rhizome. Hence, adrak halwa was created, and it became the Nawab's favourite. The Rampuri adrak halwa is still a speciality one may find at the local halwais. Amanat Bhai's shop offers the adrak halwa along with the aloe vera halwa, to cater to the latest health fad, though the amount of ghee and sugar in these halwas cannot be healthy by any stretch of imagination! The adrak halwa at Amanat bhai's shop has the base of halwa sohan—using samnak and semolina—with ginger paste added in the middle of the cooking process. It tastes like a variation of halwa sohan. Aloe vera halwa simply substitutes ginger with aloe vera. The old cookbooks as well as the recipe followed in Rampur households do not use samnak flour in the adrak halwa. Ground ginger cooked in milk forms the base of the halwa. Some recipes advice blanching the ginger before grinding it to reduce the sharp taste. The old texts are emphatic in their advocacy of using young ginger so there are no fibres to spoil the texture; old ginger contributes to coarse texture and a distinct aftertaste.

I tried out a recipe for adrak halwa shared by Muneeza Shamsie which used to be cooked at her home in Karachi. It adviced blanched and ground ginger cooked with a lot of ghee and cream. After three hours of cooking, it turned out to be creamy and rich with very little aftertaste. The opinion was divided on the adrak halwa. Some loved the gingery sweet while others declared that it tasted like hakim's majoon (medicine)!

Zarda is an all-time favourite Rampuri sweet served at weddings and banquets. I can never understand the logic of serving zarda or any form of sweet rice along with pulao; a savoury rice dish and sweet rice is just too rice dominant a feast for me. Possibly, Rampur being a rice-growing belt prompted an effusion of rice dishes, most of them picked up from ancient Mughal and Indo-Persian cuisine. Safeda is a sweet rice, which is white in colour—hence the name—and is cooked in sugar, five times the amount of rice. Each grain of rice has the sheen of the sugar syrup. Zarda, on the other hand, is less sweet and is dyed zard (yellow) with saffron. It is sometimes also called muzaffar. Nowadays, food grade colour is used instead of saffron. Begum Noor Bano recalls that the rice for zarda and safeda was brought from the Tanda tehsil of Rampur and was matured for ten years to be able to absorb the large amounts of sugar. We now have, at best, two-year-old rice, hence double the quantity of sugar is all we can aspire to. To make matters simpler, the cooks today use parboiled hybrid rice, which I find a bit too firm, almost plasticky and with zero aroma.

I like the garnish of fried dry fruits on zarda, so I generally take a tiny bite, but my son loves it. I cooked zarda once, very reluctantly; I find this dish illogical. Sensing my distaste, the rice settled down to a sweet, benign mush. It requires skill to keep the rice firm, well-cooked but never soggy despite the blitzkrieg of high ratio of sweet syrup. On the other hand, it should not go to the other end of the spectrum and stiffen up.

Besides zarda and safeda, Begum Jahanara mentions the dar e bahisht (the gateway to heaven) in *Remembrance of Days Past*. It is also described in old cookbooks. In one cookbook, it is written as 'durr e bahisht' (pearl of heaven). Amanat Bhai's grandson says he sometimes makes the dar e bahisht for the members of the royal family on special occasions. It is an almond and sugar based sweet, shaped like a very thick and large barfi. It is a difficult sweet to cook because the pastry of almond flour, sugar and milk has to be cooked to a point when the surface bubbles into holes—the jaali point. At that precise time, it is taken off the heat, spread on a flat tray and cooled. Then it is cut into about two-inch squares. It is the crisp flakiness of the jaali that is difficult to achieve. I have only heard of and read descriptions of this sweet and I'm assuming that if the crucial point is missed, the texture and taste change. Maybe it is the arduous cooking procedure or the expense of preparing the dish dovetailed with the fall in its demand that led to the discontinuation of the sweet by the local halwais and the eventual 'forgetting'. There are several variations of the dar e bahisht as described in old cookbooks—pistachios, chickpea flour, rose petals and coconut dar e bahisht—that offered several gateways to heaven where none exists now.

My husband often speaks of a forgotten sweet called shaakh e tallahi, specially cooked for the family by Laddan khansama sometime in the 1960s. Laddan was the sweetmeat expert in the royal kitchens. My husband recalls that the sweet was a long rectangle, like a shaakh or branch of a tree. At that time, each piece cost a hundred rupees, which is astronomical.

Jahanara Begum writes that shaakh e tallahi was like a roti made with sugar and saffron and was yellow in colour. A few other sweetmeats referred to in cookbooks, memoirs and oral history include nan e santara (a flat cake flavoured with orange juice and orange peel) qurmay (an oval pastry filled with nuts) and quamaq (a small samosa filled with nuts and dipped in syrup). Princess Naghat also recalls the halwa seb or apple halwa made of apple puree and khoya cooked in milk, halwa e baeza or egg halwa prepared with egg yolks cooked over coal fire and the diamond-shaped sweet called lauz e Jahangiri. The latter was probably of Mughal origin named after Emperor Jahangir. Tunki-nimish was Princess Naghat's favourite sweet, and it also finds mention in Jahanara Begum's memoirs. Nimish is an Awadhi sweet created from layers of sweet milk froth which is kept outdoors at night to set. It is eaten with tunki, a small, crisp wheat biscuit. Princess Naghat Abedi recalls that her mother, Sakeena Begum had persuaded Laddan to share his secret recipes with the princess. Laddan had agreed as the princess was a daughter of the house—as opposed to a daughter-in-law—and the precious recipes were revealed and duly noted down.

In the late '60s and '70s, the elite classes were struggling to survive by selling off their lands as the loss of the privy purse in 1971 had strapped the royalty of cash. One of the casualties of the resulting parsimony was cuisine, the most vulnerable facet of culture in times of crisis. Thus, the more expensive dishes were excluded from the royal menu and eventually forgotten.

In the 1960s, the last years of grand Rampur cuisine, my husband and his brother attended a royal banquet with their grandfather, Ameer Ahmad Khan, who was the chief secretary to Nawab Sayed Murtaza Ali Khan at that time. The distinguished gentleman kept an eagle eye on his young wards. It was a buffet, and as one of the boys reached for what looked like a kabab to go with the poori, Ameer Ahmad Khan abandoned his circle and pounced on the errant grandson and took away his plate. 'Idiot! This is hubaabi not kabab,' he hissed. Hubaabi was a deep-fried flat cake dipped in sugar syrup and looked like a round kabab. I believe the poor boy, too shy to get another plate, came home hungry. The episode became a part of family food story. Clearly, by the 1960s, some of these sweets were confined exclusively to the royal tables and unrecognizable by the ordinary populace of Rampur. Hubaabi, made of refined flour, sugar, milk and ghee required a perfect khameer (yeast) to rise or it would become flat while frying. Mangochi (the sweet moong dumplings), sheer badey, akbariyan, gosh e feel—desserts which were once available at the corner halwai shops are now all sweet, unremembered words.

Sweetmeats with secret ingredients, the disguise, was an important play at the dinner table—an art emulated from the Awadhi cuisine, which was taken to gastronomic heights in the hands of the Rampuri khansamas; so there were meat halwa, bitter gourd or karela halwa, garlic kheer and even meat gulab jamuns! These oddities earned the khansamas high praise and rewards. Some khansamas cook these incognito dishes even today and have added to the repertoire by fashioning halwas from neem leaves, garlic, turmeric etc.

Adrak Halwa

Ginger halwa is a winter speciality of Rampur. I believe the style of cooking this halwa has changed over the years as cooks try to expunge the pungent gingery taste. This recipe was followed in my grandmother's Rampur home.

Ingredients

1/2 kg young ginger roots
2 cups milk
1 1/2-2 cups sugar (or as per taste)
1 1/2-2 cups ghee
1 cup cream
2 cups khoya
1/2 cup almonds, blanched and made into a paste
10 green cardamoms, powdered
1/2 tsp kewra water
1 tsp saffron
1 pinch of flour

For the garnish

1 cup chopped almonds, raisins and chironji

Method

1. Wash and peel the ginger. It should not be fibrous, or it will spoil the halwa. Blanch it in boiling water for a few minutes and grind it (when cooled) into a fine paste in a mixer-grinder.

2. Heat the ghee for tempering. Now, add the cardamom powder and stir it. Add 1 cup of milk and a pinch of flour in the ghee. Cook it for 1 minute. Sieve it and set it aside.

3. In a pan, cook the ginger paste with 1/4 cup of milk; keep it on simmer, stirring intermittently. Add some more milk and continue to cook. The ginger should be tender. Add the sugar and cook for 5 minutes till it dissolves.

4. When it starts bubbling, add the khoya and cream. Cook it for another 5 minutes.

5. Add the almond paste. Continue to sauté it till it acquires a golden colour.

6. Pour half of the ghee-and-milk tempering on the halwa and sauté it until it leaves the sides, and the ghee is visible. Pour in the rest of the ghee. The sautéing might take about 1/2 hour. When it changes colour, add saffron and kewra water.

Safeda / Sweet Rice

Safeda has become an essential dish at all reception banquets. People add candied fruits and even khoya balls to add colour to the white rice, especially if they want to make the dish less expensive.

Ingredients

400 gm parboiled rice (sela chawal)
3 cups sugar (or as per taste)

1/2 cup ghee
1 cup milk
6-8 green cardamoms
2 black cardamoms
1 tsp kewra water
1 lemon
1 cup dry fruits—chopped raisins, almonds and cashews

Method

1. Wash the rice thoroughly till the water runs clear.
2. Make sugar syrup by cooking the sugar in 1/2 cup of milk and 2 tbsp of water. When the sugar dissolves and the syrup starts boiling, remove the scum from the top.
3. In a large pan, boil about 2 litres of water. Add 2-3 green cardamoms and lemon juice. Add the rice and allow it to boil till it is almost done and the grains are firm. Drain the rice in a colander and keep it aside.
4. Empty out the pan. Put the rice in with half of the sugar syrup and set it on simmer; let the rice absorb the syrup. Then add the rest of the syrup.
5. Heat the ghee in a frying pan and fry the dry fruits for a bit. Pour the ghee on the rice and put on dum by sealing the pan with dough or wet cloth. Let it simmer for 10 minutes till it is done.

Zarda

This is cooked in the same way as safeda, except two
teaspoons of saffron and yellow food colouring are used
when boiling the rice.

Andey Ka Halwa

I remember andey ka halwa being prepared every winter
from farm eggs and stored in large bowls at my Nani's place.
She was very particular about obliterating the egg smell by
using green cardamoms.

Ingredients

4 egg yolks
2 cups cream
1 1/4 cup sugar (or as per taste)
1 1/2 cup ghee
3 cups milk
6-8 green cardamoms
2 black cardamoms
1 cup almonds, blanched and made into a paste
1-2 tsp kewra water
1 tsp green cardamom powder
1 tsp saffron
1 pinch of flour

1/2 cup pistachios, for garnishing
Silver filigree or warq, for decoration

Method

1. Mix ghee, cardamoms, 1/2 cup of milk and a pinch of flour. Cook on high heat for 1 minute. Cool and strain it.
2. Soak the saffron in 1/4 cup of warm milk.
3. Strain the 2 cups of cream.
4. Beat the egg yolks well. Add sugar to it and stir till the sugar dissolves.
5. Add half of all three—saffron, cream and almond paste and mix them well.
6. Add half of the cooled ghee and continue to whip.
7. Put it on very low heat and keep stirring it. Slow cooking on coals is the best.
8. After some time, it will start thickening. Keep stirring till it has a halwa-like consistency.
9. Pour in 1 cup of milk and mix it.
10. Add the rest of the ghee and keep cooking.
11. Add a splash of milk and continue to stir it. Repeat it thrice till all the milk is used and the halwa takes on an almond colour. The ghee should become visible on the sides and the liquid should evaporate.
12. Add kewra water, cardamom powder and saffron. Stir it well and remove from the heat.
13. Garnish the dish with pistachios and decorate with silver filigree warq.

Fourteen

Akhadas and Libidinous Fare

Saim Khan could easily have followed the long line of pehelwani (wrestling) tradition of his family. Tall and muscular, he has all the physical characteristics of a wrestler, like most of the boys of his extended family. With the Pathan suit and Afghani cap he dons, he wouldn't look out of place in a Kabul bazaar. Saim, a twenty-six-year-old science graduate, hovers undecided between the akhada (wrestling ring) tradition and the pull of the world outside. As his former teacher, I had developed a fondness for this big, gentle boy; scolded him, counselled him and followed the videos he posted on his YouTube channel, Saimcoolestkhan. Most of these videos are about the famed Akhada Sohrab Khan founded by and named after his great grandfather, Sohrab Khan. I have persisted in nudging him to pursue his career goals, fulfil the promise of his school years even as I see him sinking into the comfort zone of life around the akhada. His siblings and cousins have all left Rampur to take up careers in

Middle East and Australia. They often cajole him to take the plunge, tempting him with anecdotes and pictures of their plush lifestyle abroad but Saim is stuck in the limbo of small-town life where everyone knows him and his ancestry. He cannot think of giving up his identity and history to live an anonymous life abroad.

'When you are born a Rampur hound, you cannot become a poodle,' he tells me. Moreover, he says he cannot abandon his parents in their old age. I counter his bluff, telling him that his parents are still young, that he will regret his decision. I have seen many of my students slip into the contented familiarity of Rampuri life, giving excuses till it is too late and they have lost their confident, promising sheen; the subject of their conversation has veered from success stories and career possibilities to the immediate and local. I don't want that to happen to Saim. He is a bright, sincere kid.

Akhada Sohrab Khan is one of the oldest akhadas in Rampur which trains young men in the art of wrestling and prepares them for regional wrestling matches. It was established by Tafazzul Khan, a famous wrestler from Bareilly. Sometime in the 1860s or 1870s, Nawab Sayed Kalbe Ali Khan had invited Tafazzul Khan to set up an akhada and had given him land for the same. Oral history says that Tafazzul Khan had unintentionally killed a British official at a wrestling match and had decided to leave Bareilly, which was governed by the British, and settle in the princely state of Rampur. Tafazzul had Rohilla Pathan antecedents and traced his ancestry back to Dost Khalid Ghani Khan of Swat. This must have contributed to his acceptability in Rampur as most Pathan families of Rampur had migrated from Roh—the Swat and

Bajaur area called the Pakhtunkhwa—presently located in
Pakistan-Afghanistan border highlands.

An interesting anecdote about Tafazzul's dedication and
skill is narrated by Prof. Agha Ashar Lucknowi in *Gama
Gamak*, the biography of the world famous Gama Pehelwan.
Once, when Tafazzul was engaged in his early morning
exercise routine in front of his house, Shah sahib, a faqir
from Punjab, happened to pass by. Shah sahib stopped and
smiled at him. Tafazzul invited him to his house where Shah
sahib stayed for two or three days. He observed the wrestler
closely and impressed by his dedication, Shah sahib taught
him some dund (sit-ups) and mugda (wooden club) exercises.
The next day Shah sahib disappeared. They found a piece
of gold buried under some ashes in his room. The story
goes that Tafazzul continued to exercise following Shah's
techniques and his body became lean and muscular. A year
later, Shah sahib returned and was happy to see the results of
the exercises on Tafazzul's body. He said he wanted to be sure
that Tafazzul could be an apt pupil. It is said that Shah then
revealed the principles of exercise and their effects on the
body and demonstrated some secret exercises too. He asked
Tafazzul to make a 12-inch-by-8-inch naali (depression) in the
ground and instructed him in the technique of deep push-ups
for wrestlers. He also taught Tafazzul to make wooden clubs
of six kilograms each with specific dimensions for the mugda
exercises. Even today, the best wooden clubs for exercising are
made in Rampur. The level of expertise imparted to Tafazzul
was such that he could shape and tone each muscle of the
body using Shah's techniques. Before he had learnt these
secrets, Tafazzul's body was fatty despite exercise. The akhada

garnered a reputation for sculpting a lean body. Of the gold found in the room, Shah said he knew the secrets of alchemy and could turn certain elements into gold. 'I have gifted you the secret element to make gold,' he told Tafazzul.

Tafazzul's son, Sohrab Khan, after whom the akhada and the mohalla are known today, became famous all over India and abroad for his wrestling and exercises. In 1898 Gama Pehelwan came to stay at the akhada to sculpt his abdomen. By that time Tafazzul had gone blind and Sohrab was in top form. Gama wanted to take Sohrab and some other wrestlers with him to Lahore to be a part of his team of wrestlers. Tafazzul refused saying, 'You won't be able to keep my wrestlers lean. Besides, Sohrab is my only son and must maintain the traditions of the akhada.'

The special deep naali push-ups and wooden-club exercises are unique to Rampur akhadas. Due to the wrestlers' knowledge of the muscles of the body, the akhadas were also traditional physiotherapy centres. Asghar Shadani writes in *Ahwal e Riyasat e Rampur* that people with muscle weakness or paralysis visited the akhadas and were admitted there for treatment. With exercise and proper diet, they were able to walk home. Gama pehelwan said in an interview, 'Ustad Sohrab Khan can treat deficiency in any part of the body with his exercises.'

Sohrab Khan Akhada is not only known for its style of exercising and wrestling, but also for the instructions of special diet for the wrestlers and for patients with muscle weakness. A typical day at the akhada begins after the early morning fajr prayers. The exercise routine is carried out in a mud-floor courtyard with naalis for push-ups; wooden poles, resting on the walls, for squats; and several wood clubs for the famous mugda exercises. There is one naali in the courtyard called Gama ki naali where the legendary wrestler did his push-ups more than a century ago. The courtyard is divided into three sections for different grades or levels of learning of the students. Under an ancient khaprail (mud tiled) roof is the wrestling arena with soft, dark mud to practice the different bunds (wrestling poses). The pehelwans are massaged with special medicinal oils on the stone platforms to tone and relax the muscles. It's a 'male only' domain and females can only have a sneak preview of the akhada on YouTube.

After the morning exercises, the wrestlers are supposed to have badam doodh (skimmed milk mixed with almond paste). They are advised to eat only lean meat—mutton or chicken—in the form of thin gravy cooked in pure ghee or as soup for both the meals with wheat roti. They cannot eat rice or any form of chiknai (fat). They have to drink the protein-rich sattu thandai (roasted gram flour drink)—a great alternative to the synthetic protein shakes that modern day bodybuilders are fond of.

The akhada still trains wrestlers for state level matches but very few wrestlers are dedicated to the sport. Young men generally come for bodybuilding and use the akhada as an affordable alternative to the gym. Saim tells me there is a lot of competition and trouble from other akhadas. The last of the great wrestlers from the line of Sohrab Khan was Barzu Ustad who passed away two years ago. His son was called over from Australia and symbolically given the charge of the akhada at a dastgari (turban tying) ceremony. He returned to Australia and his brother manages the akhada now. Saim helps his cousin out. He cannot reconcile himself to leaving the familiar for the unknown and clings to familial love as an excuse. I can see him gaining weight, and I can see the oncoming confident swagger of a man with a famous ancestry. Soon I shall stop speaking to him about career prospects abroad, IELTS exams and other possibilities.

Ustad Sohrab Khan's Murgh / Mutton Yakhni

It is said that Ustad Sohrab ate the yakhni soup of one whole rooster in the morning along with 250 grams almonds, 250 grams pistachios and 1 litre of milk.

Ingredients

(For 2 litres yakhni)
400 gm chicken or mutton
1 cup curd (optional)
1 medium-sized onion, roughly diced
3 cloves garlic, finely diced
1 inch ginger, finely diced
2 tsp black peppercorns
3-4 green cardamoms
3-4 cloves
3-4 bay leaves
3-4 whole red or yellow chillies
1 tbsp pure ghee

3 litres of water
Salt to taste

Method

1. In a pressure cooker, heat the ghee. Add cardamoms, cloves and peppercorns. When they start crackling, add the garlic.
2. Put the chicken pieces into it and sauté.
3. Add onions, ginger, chillies and water and bring to a rolling boil. Then lower the flame and simmer. Pour in the curd.
4. Pressure cook on simmer till the meat falls off the bones and the bones become soft. In a normal pan, it takes about 4 hours to cook this dish.
5. Strain the soup. Add back the meat pieces into the soup.
6. Serve it hot.

Guddi or Trotter Soup[1]

This soup has magical restorative properties for convalescence. It is a practice in my family to serve it for debilitating weakness, after childbirth or post-operatively

---

[1] It is a versatile soup. If an inch of ginger, a potato, a cup of curd and dried red chillies are added while boiling the bones, it becomes Kashmiri-style yakhni soup. It can be eaten with bread, rice or roti.

because of its anti-inflammatory properties (effects of glycerine and proline). It is a strength-giving winter soup for all as it contains calcium, phosphorous, magnesium that strengthen the bones. I drink it every winter for the much-needed collagen. This is a recipe from our old retainer, Ismail Bhai, who nursed generations of our family through various ailments.

Ingredients

1 kg knuckle and trotter bones
2 tsp black peppercorns
3–4 green cardamoms
3–4 cloves
3–4 bay leaves
1 inch piece cinnamon
Salt to taste

Method

1. Wash the bones thoroughly. Put them in a pan or a pressure cooker along with cardamoms, cloves, cinnamon, bay leaves and peppercorns. The use of spices is optional; they are used to mask the smell.
2. Add enough water so that it covers the bones and stands 3 inches above the bones. Add the required amount of salt.
3. Let the soup simmer in the pan for 5 hours or in the pressure cooker for about an hour till the bones crumble.

4. It is best to have the soup without sieving and chew on the bones.
5. Serve it hot. The leftover broth can be stored in the freezer and served every day.

Hareera

A drink made from the paste of dry fruits generally given to new mothers. This is a traditional recipe from my aunt, Fareeda Khan.

Ingredients

(For one cup)
4–5 almonds
4–5 cashews
4–5 walnut kernels
5 pistachios
10 raisins
1 tsp of each kind of melon or maghaz seeds (watermelon, cantaloupe, pumpkin and cucumber)
1 tsp poppy or khashkhash seeds
1/4 inch piece of dried ginger (saunth)
1 green cardamom
1 tsp ghee
1 cup milk
Sugar, honey or jaggery (as per taste) (optional)

Method

1. Soak all the dry fruits, saunth and the seeds overnight or at least for 3–4 hours. Grind them in a mixer–grinder into a paste.[2]

2. Add 1 cup of milk or, if lactose intolerant, add 1 cup of water to the paste.

3. In a pan, heat the ghee and add the cardamoms till they start crackling.

4. Add the mixture and bring to boil.

5. Serve it hot.

---

[2] Tip: make the paste in bulk and freeze it.

Fifteen

Spirituality, Sacrifice and Sufi Mazars

'Case hopeless. Come and collect your patient.'

The telegram sent by Dr Nigam of Lucknow Medical College devastated the father. His beloved son, and my grandfather, Abdul Jabbar Khan, a young engineer in the service of Nawab Sayed Raza Ali Khan, was critical after an appendix operation. This was the time before antibiotics entered the scene; my grandfather's stomach filled with septic pus was bound with muslin cloth and his feet were raised to reduce the swelling. Relatives and friends rushed to Rampur to say their goodbyes. Nawab Sayed Raza Ali Khan granted leave to all those who wanted to meet the popular riyasat engineer for the last time.

The family lore goes that the father prayed fervently for his son's life and that night he had a dream that Hazrat Ali was taking him to his dying son's bedside. He turned to Hazrat Ali and said, 'Maula, my son is dying. Please save him.' Hazrat Ali touched the boy's swollen stomach and said, 'He shall be cured.'

Miraculously, Jabbar Khan started recovering but the father became ill. Oral family history has it that the father had offered his life in exchange for his young son's in a Babur–Humayun-style death-wish exchange. The father passed away and the son survived. The news of Ghani Khan's death was kept a secret from the recovering son. The doting stepmother, the formidable Kaptanni Bibi, wore colourful clothes instead of the widow's white when she visited her stepson and forbade anyone to mention the death. She didn't even confine herself for the iddat period prescribed for widows.[1]

It was when my grandfather returned to Rampur that he realized that his father was no more. Heartbroken, he went to his father's grave, nestled next to the ancestral house, put his head on the mud mound and wept. From that day on, he declared that his father was his pir (spiritual guide) and he owed his life to the miracle wrought by the pious gentleman. All his life, he observed the death anniversary of his pir and father as a three-day mini urs,[2] with all-night qawwali performances by Murli and other well-known qawwals of the day. My mother remembers watching a faqir enter into haal—a trance-like state—and start dancing and beating his head on the floor in ecstasy as the qawwali notes rose to their alliterative crescendo. Golden-hued taar curry with tandoori roti was distributed to the attendees and the poor. On the third day, a chadar was laid on the grave while Murli, with the

---

[1] Iddat is the waiting period for widows and divorced women during which time they cannot remarry. It is also to establish the paternity of a child if the woman is pregnant. In the Indian subcontinent, Muslim women confine themselves to their homes and do not travel.

[2] Urs, derived from the Arabic 'urs' or wedding, celebrates the cosmic union of the Sufi saint with God after the former's death.

harmonium tied to his waist, stood and sang the famous Rang qawwali by Amir Khusrau:

Aaj rang hai hey maa rang hai ri,
Merey Khwaja ke ghar rang hai ri.

(Today there is celestial colour, O mother,
What glowing colours at my beloved Khwaja's home.)

Sufi saints' death anniversaries—believed to be their cosmic union with Allah—are celebrated as 'urs' on different days in the various Sufi shrines in Rampur. Stories of their miracles or kashka are narrated in oral history. The yearly urs at Baghdadi Sahab and Hafiz Jamal dargahs draw huge crowds. Hafiz Jamal was greatly respected by Nawab Sayed Kalbe Ali Khan, and the latter is buried near the saint in the hope of receiving spiritual blessings of his pir. Both my grandfather-in-law and grandmother-in-law are also buried there. Generally, women from our family are not expected to visit graves and mazars. I visited the dargah of Hafiz Jamal and met the mujabir (maulvi-in-charge) as part of my research. The saint's tomb is a beautiful domed structure and there is a smaller tomb of Nawab Sayed Kalbe Ali Khan next to it.

Another famous dargah is of Baghdadi Sahab, which is close to my ancestral house. Baghdadi Sahab had settled in Rampur right after the inception of Rampur in 1774 and was highly revered by Nawab Sayed Faizullah Khan (ruled 1774–1794), the founder of Rampur. My great grandfather, Ghani Khan's tomb says that he was devoted to Baghdadi Sahab, observed the holy day of gyarahween shareef at the shrine and passed away on that auspicious day. During urs at Baghdadi Sahab's mazar, a special dal is served in clay bowls with khameeri roti to all the devotees. It is a humble dish, a favourite of the Sufi saint. My friends, Muslim Bhai and Sitara Bhabhi, live next to the mazar and are devoted to the saint. They get the chana dal prepared at home in large deghs and distribute it on six days of Muharram culminating with the final day of urs on fourteenth of Muharram, the day the saint left the mortal world. Currently, they are writing a biography on the life and teachings of the saint.

I visited Muslim Bhai's house on the last day of urs, two years ago. The dargah was so crowded that I couldn't visit the shrine next door. As I was leaving the house, their gardener came in with a chakotra (pomelo) plant. Sitara Bhabhi didn't have space for the citrus in her garden and offered it to me. Coincidentally, I had cut down the pomelo tree in my house a few days ago because it was endangering the compound wall. As I am fond of the fruit, I was meaning to plant a new tree soon. Maybe it was a sign, or a tiny miracle. My friends were convinced it would bring me luck. The young tree now stands in my fruit patch, sturdy and beautiful, and I await its first fruits.

Shah Baghdadi's Dal

Sitara Bhabhi attributes the success of her three sons to the blessings of Baghdadi Sahab. I remember she used to get her house locked up from outside when the children had their exams to dissuade visitors. This is a recipe from her.

Ingredients

200 gm chana dal
3–4 tbsp ghee
1 tsp turmeric powder
1 tsp red chilli powder
1 tsp coriander powder
1 medium-sized onion, finely diced
1 tbsp garlic paste
1 tsp ginger paste (optional)
1 tsp garam masala powder
1 tsp salt (or as per taste)

For the garnish

1 inch ginger, julienned
5–6 green chillies, finely chopped
1 bunch of coriander leaves, chopped

Method

1. Wash and soak the dal for at least 2 to 3 hours.
2. Boil the dal with turmeric, coriander and red chilli powders, ginger–garlic pastes and salt till the dal turns soft. If a pressure cooker is used, add 2 cups of water and boil. Add some extra water to make it runny. Mash the dal

with a flat wooden spoon till the texture becomes thick and grainy. Add the garam masala.

3. Fry the onions in ghee till golden brown and temper the dal. Set the dal in clay bowls. Garnish the dish before serving.

Huzoor Pasand Dal

This was a favourite dal of the Nawabs and is served with qorma curry, though it can be savoured as a single dish to be eaten with roti.

Ingredients

150 gm white urad dal
2–3 tbsp ghee
4 dried red or yellow chillies, chopped into 1/2 inch pieces
1 medium-sized onion, finely diced
1 cup milk (optional)
1 tsp cumin
1 inch piece of ginger, julienned
2–3 bay leaves
2–3 cloves
1 black cardamom
1 tsp salt (or as per taste)

For the garnish

3–4 green chillies, finely chopped

Method

1. Wash and soak the dal 1-2 hours before cooking.
2. The dal should be cooked in a pan rather than a pressure cooker so that it doesn't become too soft. Add milk and 1 cup of water to dal and cook.
3. When it starts boiling, add salt, red chillies, zeera, spices and half of the ginger. Let it simmer till it becomes soft and the water dries up. It should look like boiled rice with each grain separate.
4. Before serving, fry the onions in ghee and temper the dal. Set it in a bowl. Garnish the dish with chillies and ginger.

Kewati Dal

This is a mixed dal and has five kinds of pulses. I personally do not use moong dal in it though several people do. The proportion of dal may be altered as per taste.

Ingredients

50 gm white urad dal
50 gm arhar dal

50 gm split red masoor dal
50 gm chana dal
1 tsp turmeric power
1 tsp red chilli powder
1 inch ginger, julienned
3–4 green chillies, chopped
1 tsp salt (or as per taste)

For tempering

8 cloves of garlic, finely chopped
4–5 tbsp ghee
1 medium-sized onion, finely diced

Method

1. Mix and wash the pulses. Put them into a pressure cooker with 2 cups of water. Add the turmeric powder, chilli powder, ginger and salt and cook them till the pulses are soft. The texture should be between too thick and too runny. If it turns too thick, add some boiled water to get the required consistency.

2. Heat the ghee in a pan. Add the garlic and stir them till they change colour. Add the onions and fry them until they turn golden, then temper the dal and serve.

Chana Dal Karela

Split chickpea pulses cooked with bitter gourd. This is a
recipe from Parveen Apa.

Ingredients

100 gm split chickpea or chana dal
1/2 kg medium-sized bitter gourd or karela
1 tsp turmeric powder
1 tsp red chilli powder
1 tsp coriander powder
1 tsp dried mango powder
1 medium-sized onion, finely diced
2-3 tbsp mustard oil

Method

1. Soak the chana dal for 3–4 hours.
2. Scrape the rugged surface of the bitter gourds, cut them
   lengthwise and remove the seeds from inside. Now
   rub them with salt, rolling the gourds in the palm and
   squeezing out the bitter juice. Soak the gourds in salt
   water for 1 hour. Drain the water and wash the gourds. If
   the gourd is too bitter, you can even boil them.
3. In a pan, put the lentils with all the masalas. Pour the oil
   and place the gourds on top of the lentils.
4. Add 1 cup of water and let it simmer till the lentils are
   done. It should not be mushy. It should have the texture
   of boiled rice. I prefer to boil the gourds in the pan instead

of a pressure cooker because they tend to get too soft in the pressure cooker.

Urad Dal Gosht

My mother is not fond of this preparation of meat cooked in whole urad dal. It is considered rustic and is served at weddings in the villages around Rampur. My cook, Akhtar Bhai who hails from a village, loves to cook it. This is his recipe.

Ingredients

250 gm whole urad dal
250 gm meat[3]
3 onions, finely diced
1 tbsp ginger paste
1 tbsp garlic paste
1 tsp turmeric powder
1 1/2–2 tsp red chilli powder
1 tsp coriander powder
1 cup ghee or refined oil
6 bay leaves

---

[3] The amount of meat can be increased to 500 gm. In that case, all the masalas that are put into the meat will be doubled. However, ginger and garlic will be 1 and 1/2 tbsp each.

5 black cardamoms
5 cloves
1 mace crushed
1/2 nutmeg crushed
5 green cardamoms
2 tsp garam masala powder
2 tsp aromatic garam masalas
Salt to taste

Method

1. Boil the lentils in a pressure cooker with 1tsp turmeric powder, mace, nutmeg and 3 bay leaves. Cook them till the lentils are soft. The texture should be something between thick and runny. Use the back of a spoon to mash the lentils. Whole grains should not be visible; it should be homogenous. Set it aside.
2. In a pressure cooker, heat the oil and fry the onions till they turn golden. Tip: If mustard oil is used, it should be heated till the smell evaporates.
3. Add the whole garam masalas (cardamoms, cloves and bay leaves).
4. Add the meat, ginger–garlic pastes, the remaining turmeric powder, coriander and red chilli powder and sauté them on low heat till the oil separates.
5. Pour 1 cup of water and pressure cook till the meat is tender.
6. Add the lentils to the meat and bring to boil. Mix it well and let it simmer till the required consistency is achieved.

Check the salt. Add the garam masala powder and the aromatic powder.

7. Serve it hot with rice or roti.

Baurani

This eggplant and yoghurt dish is basically from Afghanistan where it is called Borani Banjan. We have a slightly different version of it in Rampur. It is served with pulao.

Ingredients

3–4 medium aubergines
2 cups thick curd, preferably hung curd
4–5 garlic cloves, crushed
2–3 green chillies, chopped
1 tsp red chilli powder
1/2 tsp turmeric powder (optional)
1/2 cup oil
1 tbsp mint leaves, chopped
Salt to taste

Method

1. Wash and cut the aubergines into 1 mm thick slices. Sprinkle them with 1/2 tsp red chilli powder, turmeric powder and salt.

2. Heat the oil in a frying pan and shallow fry the slices on low heat. Turn them and continue to fry till they are brown and soft. Drain them and put them on kitchen tissue to remove excess water.
3. Prepare the curd by adding half of the crushed garlic, salt and chillies. Whisk the mixture.
4. In a flat-bottomed serving dish, put a layer of fried aubergines. Spread the curd on top.

Heat a tablespoon of ghee or oil and fry the crushed garlic till they are golden. Temper the curd with it. Before serving, garnish the dish with mint leaves and green chillies.

Acknowledgements

I'm deeply thankful to the librarians at the Rampur Raza Library who helped me in accessing the cookbook manuscripts and assisted in the translations. A special thanks to Mr Isbah Khan who looked through ancient Persian dictionaries and spoke to old-timers to help me make sense of the recipes and the notations for the measurements. The old khansamas of Rampur are the repositories of royal food stories and recipes. They were happy to help me and share their knowledge of some forgotten dishes. Their expertise also enabled me to decode and practically apply the recipes I had translated. I'm indebted to Majid khansama from the lineage of royal khansamas, and Chef Suroor, a first generation khansama who brought their ideas and skills to my kitchen and shared their recipes.

I'm blessed with a number of aunts—from my family, my husband's family and through a network of relationships that are considered close in Rampur—who are inheritors of generations of delicious quotidian and celebratory recipes. I turned to them, and they were delighted to share their recipes and family food lore with great love, laughter and generosity. I'm deeply thankful to Begum Noor Bano for her lovely food stories and her list of forgotten foods to work on. To Princess Naghat Abedi for sharing her memories of the royal dining table and images of her resplendent Nauroz offering. I will always be beholden to the project 'Forgotten Food: Culinary Memory, Local Heritage and Lost Agricultural Varieties in India'—funded by the Arts and Humanities Research Council in the United Kingdom and executed under the lead of the University of Sheffield—which gave me the resources and the confidence to carry out my research into the culinary archives; and to Professor Siobhan Lambert Hurley for her inspiring guidance and for making all this a possibility. To Professor Duncan Cameron for making the resurrection of heritage rice a possibility. To my editors, Meru, Aparna, Shaoni and Shreya, for appreciating my work and giving me the confidence to ramble on and to Antra for the brilliant cover design. I am thankful to the team at Penguin Random House India for making this book possible. To Kanishka for always being there for me.

To my children Nadir, Gaeti and Rahima for suffering through my cooking experiments and encouraging me; to my husband for connecting me to old-timers, calling over old khansamas and exploring the qila and ancient kothis with me, always beside me in my quest. Mamma with her unerring taste and her devotion to Rampuri food. To Taran for her writerly advice and her efforts at making me politically correct, and to Asad. To Rana Safvi for her support.

At the end, this book is for my beloved Nani Amma who taught me to appreciate good food, to detail the nuances of taste and identify the shortcomings of dishes without stirring from the dining table. I think that's the life I will always want—delicious food on the table with the least effort.